Brief Heroes
& Histories

Other books by Barbara Holland
in Common Reader Editions

One's Company
In Private Life

Brief Heroes & Histories

BARBARA HOLLAND

edited by Chris Carruth & Thomas Meagher

A COMMON READER EDITION
THE AKADINE PRESS

Brief Heroes & Histories

A COMMON READER EDITION published 1998
by The Akadine Press, Inc.

Many of these articles appeared previously in *Smithsonian, Discovery Channel Monthly, A & E Monthly,* and *Mid-Atlantic Country.*

A COMMON READER EDITION and fountain colophon are trademarks of The Akadine Press, Inc.

ISBN 1-888173-31-9

10 9 8 7 6 5 4 3 2 1

Contents

Introduction

HOW HISTORY HAS LOST ITS LUSTER. I remember quite fondly foraging as a child through the local library, consuming biographies and historical novels as if they were the ripest berries learning had ever tasted. Their protagonists were larger than life, the adventures they experienced noble and impassioned, the events that turned upon their actions important enough to decide the fates of nations, ideals, souls. Paul Revere and Francis Marion (the "Swamp Fox" of the American Revolution), Joan of Arc and Garibaldi, Caesar and Cicero, the fierce soldiers of Sparta and the warriors of Troy, Mahatma Gandhi and the North American martyrs – all entered my head clothed in story: how dashing and dangerous, engrossing and exciting seemed every plot the past had spun.

The costumes of my imagination, I later discovered, were not always authentic, for the dress of history – as entire schools of historiography have relentlessly asserted – is more often drab than dramatic, and economic and political forces obey neither the whims nor the wisdom of the great and the good (to say nothing of the small and the pure), but move along their determined paths in ineluctable pursuit of tales less compelling than those that entertained, and enlarged, my childish mind. What's known as "human interest" has little place in the official annals of the past. Stripped of the fancy garments such sympathy bestows upon them, the most exalted heroes and heroines can seem small, mean, and in no shape to bear the burden of the ideals we wish upon them. Experts in any field are trained to be adept at such disrobing.

As a result, another kind of human interest (adult, and harassed by all sorts of mundane yet unforgiving monsters unimagined in the most comprehensive book of fairy tales) loses its bearings as it wanders through the years looking for something to read. Frightened by the overwhelming edifices of scholarship that loom over the intellectual landscape, eclipsing the beam of our still, small book lights, our desire to know hides itself between the covers of humble tomes, chastened by the obvious fact we will never know enough ("Enough for what?" we're too well-bred to ask). Curiosity itself – the true author of those juvenile books I eulogize in memory – becomes an endangered pleasure.

Which brings me, neatly if indirectly, to Barbara Holland. A few years ago, we received a package from Bluemont, Virginia; it contained a newly published volume called *Endangered Pleasures,* along with a hastily scribbled note from its author suggesting it was just the sort of book for our catalogue, A COMMON READER. She couldn't have been more correct, and we were eager to know more of her work. Correspondence traveled between Pleasantville and

Bluemont, packages arrived and departed. We found ourselves happily adding two of Barbara's books, *One's Company: Reflections on Living Alone* and *In Private Life*, to our fledgling list of COMMON READER EDITIONS. When she came to New York for a visit, we couldn't help asking if she had any stray pieces we might collect into another volume. *Brief Heroes & Histories* is the result of that query.

As Barbara explains in her afterword, the pieces gathered here are of various provenance. (As she is also quick to announce, they were all written with an eye to a paycheck: in the here and now, as another favorite writer of mine, Hubert Butler, once put it, "curiosity has no status unless it is paid.") They are the fruit of quick study rather than arduous scholarship. Nonetheless their sentences – admirable, as this author's often are, for their lucidity and offhand eloquence – recalled to me the pleasures of that childhood library where I was so eager just to find things out: any things and all things. Whether setting her prose on the trail of William Penn or Pocahontas, Robin Hood or Betsy Ross, Cleopatra or Elvis Presley, ice cream or Manifest Destiny, the history of juries or the prevalence of dueling in our not-so-distant past, Barbara Holland leads us into the wonderful wood of curiosity for no other purpose than to look around. If you're like me, you can use the air.

James Mustich, Jr.
Publisher, A COMMON READER

THE SEARCH FOR CLEOPATRA

THE CLEOPATRA STORY IS nothing if not versatile. The elements are a dramatist's dream – exotic locale, wealth beyond measuring, passion, war, conquest, tragedy. For two thousand years, however, the central character has been pushed into shapes to fit all manner of theories and themes and personal agendas.

Everyone now knows her as queen of the Nile and passion's plaything, whose bared bosom made an asp gasp when she died for love, true love. Movies are our principal source: Theda Bara, Claudette Colbert, Vivien Leigh, Elizabeth Taylor, all demonstrating what fun it was to be filthy rich in the first century B.C., spending days in enormous bathtubs and nights in scented sheets. Drinking pearls dissolved in vinegar. (Do not try this at home; it doesn't work.) Lounging around on a barge, waited on hand and foot. Sometimes the asp looks like a small price to pay for such a glamorous fling.

Hollywood's queen rests loosely on Shakespeare's, though in *Antony and Cleopatra* she's a fiercer soul, downright unhinged by love. Of course, he had to leave out her children. Everyone does. It's tough being the world's top tragic lover with four kids underfoot. Even if you can get a sitter, it doesn't look right. Every good story needs an editor.

Writing seventy years later, John Dryden in *All for Love* gives us a meeker queen, an insidious clinging vine who wails:

> There I till death will his unkindness weep;
> As harmless infants moan themselves to sleep.

Dryden tells it as the tale of a once-noble fellow who, forced to choose between love and duty, can't say no to love and gets his comeuppance, but it's worth it. His Cleo is less a ruler than an addictive substance.

In *Caesar and Cleopatra*, George Bernard Shaw has different fish to fry. His Cleopatra stands for everything lamentably un-British, and in the course of the play she evolves from a superstitious, cowardly little girl into a vengeful, bloodthirsty little girl. To underline his point he lops five years off her actual age and leaves her under the thumb of a sturdy Roman governor, forerunner of the wise and kindly British administrators of later colonies full of childish foreigners.

Everyone's story goes back to Plutarch, the first-century Greek historian, and he was torn between two stories himself. He knew people in her own part of the world who remembered her as a scholar in their own refined tradition, so unlike the ignorant, loutish Romans; a mothering goddess; a messiah sent to liberate the East from under the jackboots of Rome. On the other hand, he had the official Roman story, the queen as drunken harlot and "the wickedest woman in the world."

Octavius gave us the Roman version. As her enemy in war, her conqueror, and later when he was the emperor Augustus (clueless husband of the evil Livia in the television series, *I, Claudius*), he worked hard to write her into the record as everything scheming, treacherous, female, foreign, and, most of all, sexually rapacious.

The Romans dealt out their own lady relatives as political collateral and were shocked down to their sandal-toes by a woman who picked her own partners. Octavius started the ball rolling and pretty soon she was world-famous for sex and had romped with her household slaves until she was plumb tuckered out, besides being drunk most of the time. Somehow this same strumpet found time to threaten Rome with her nasty talents, having blinded Mark Antony with passion. She could be vanquished only by Octavius's noble self, symbol of all that was pure and manly: he alone was immune to her blandishments.

In a completely new and different twist, now taught to American schoolchildren, she's black, a helpless victim of racist Romans, not to mention racist historians. (The last time we looked she was a Macedonian Greek, but the Macedonian storytellers seem to be asleep at the switch.) The black-Cleopatra forces point out that nobody knows anything about her paternal grandmother except that she wasn't legally married to Ptolemy IX, and it stands to reason that when two people aren't legally married, one of them must be a black slave.

The Ptolemies were wicked snobs and so proud of their bloodline that they mostly married their brothers and sisters to keep it pure. When they picked mistresses, they picked upper-class Greeks. They felt so superior to the Egyptians that, after three hundred years in Alexandria, they couldn't even say "good morning" to them in their native tongue; Cleopatra was the first in her family to learn the language. You'd think, if her father's mother was a native, he'd have picked up a few words at her knee. And you'd think, if Cleopatra was the black grandchild of a slave, Octavius would have brandished it in his slanderous rantings; he called her everything else in the book.

But the point isn't whether she really *had* a black grandmother. The point is, if we say she did, it tells the tale of Africans oppressed by Europeans. Fans of the theory argue that, when it comes to history, a good story is all that matters.

Actually, where we can sniff them out, the facts make a pretty good story too.

Cleopatra VII was born in 69 B.C., third child of Ptolemy XII, called Auletes, the Flute Player. (This was probably not a nice thing to call your king. The implication is that he didn't do much else.)

Egypt was still rich but its ancient empire had been nibbled away and the natives were always restless. The Flute Player kept having to go to Rome for help in holding his throne. He may have taken Cleopatra along when she was twelve; she may have watched the Romans charge him ten thousand talents, or nearly twice Egypt's annual revenue, for military services to be rendered. This was on top of the six thousand he'd paid earlier. He had to borrow from Roman loan sharks.

Not only couldn't he control his subjects, he couldn't do a thing with his children. While he was away his eldest daughter, Tryphaena, grabbed the throne, and then after she got assassinated his second daughter, Berenice, jumped in. When he came back with Roman help, he had her executed.

Cleopatra, now the eldest, had cause to ponder. She knew Egypt needed Rome, but paying cash for help was beggaring the place. Maybe she considered a cheaper road to recruiting allies; maybe even, eventually, thumbing Egypt's nose at Rome. Certainly she learned to watch her back around her family (I suppose you could call it dysfunctional).

She seems to have found herself an education, though that clashes with Shaw's story; he tells us, "I do not feel bound to believe that Cleopatra was well educated. Her father, the illustrious Flute Blower, was not at all a parent of the Oxford professor type." Without an Oxonian father, who could possibly learn to read?

However, Cicero, who couldn't stand her, grudgingly admits she was literary and involved like him in "things that had to do with learning." The Arab historian Al-Masudi tells us she was the author of learned works, and "a princess well versed in the sciences, disposed to the study of philosophy." Plutarch says she spoke nine or ten languages, though some of her relatives barely spoke their own.

In 51 B.C., when Cleopatra was eighteen, the Flute Player died and left the kingdom to her and her ten-year-old brother (and fiancé), Ptolemy XIII. The reign got off on the wrong foot, with the Nile refusing to flood its banks for the harvest. People hid out from the tax-collector. Pothinus reared his ugly head. Pothinus was a court eunuch who'd appointed himself regent for little Ptolemy and presently managed to squeeze Cleopatra clear out of town and started giving all the orders himself.

Rome, meanwhile, was in the process of shedding its republican privileges to become an empire. An early phase involved the uneasy power-sharing device called the First Triumvirate, with Caesar, Pompey, and Crassus (a money man) jointly in charge. It wasn't Rome's brightest idea. Caesar and Pompey quarreled, Caesar defeated Pompey in Greece, Pompey took refuge in Egypt. Not wanting to harbor a loser, the Egyptians had him murdered and cut off his head and presented it to victorious Caesar when he sailed into Alexandria to collect the defunct Flute Player's debts. Pothinus had reason to hate and fear Rome. He was very likely plotting to do in Caesar, too, who took over the palace and stayed on with a guard of three thousand Roman soldiers. He couldn't take his ships and go home; the winds were unfavorable.

Cleopatra needed a secret word with him, so as we've all heard, she got herself rolled up in some bedding and had herself delivered to Caesar as merchandise. According to Plutarch, Caesar was first captivated by this proof of Cleopatra's bold wit, and afterward so overcome by the charm of her society that he made a reconciliation between her and her brother. Then he killed Pothinus. So there was Cleopatra, at the price of being briefly half-smothered in bedding, with her throne back. And of course, sleeping with Caesar, who was in his fifties and losing his hair.

How did she do it? Cleopatra's looks are one of the burning issues of the ages. European painters see her as a languishing blue-eyed blonde with nothing to wear but that asp. However, there's a coin in the British Museum with her profile on it, and she looks exactly like Abraham Lincoln before he grew a beard. Historians agree that she commissioned the coins herself and, being a woman, was vain of her looks, so this must have been downright flattering, and it launched many a nasty crack about her nose. The seventeenth-century French writer Blaise Pascal said that if it had been shorter, the whole face of the world would have been changed. However, there's no evidence that Antony was unhappy with her nose the way it was.

Or maybe it wasn't so long. Maybe she thought more of her kingdom than her vanity and wanted to scare off possible enemies by looking fierce. Considering the speed with which she corrupted Rome's top commanders, both of them widely traveled, experienced married men, it's possible she looked more like a woman and less like Mount Rushmore than she does on the coins. The second-century Greek historian Dio Cassius says she seduced Caesar because she was "brilliant to look upon . . . with the power to subjugate everyone." (She knew a few things about fixing herself up, too, and wrote a book on cosmetics full of ingredients unknown to Estée Lauder, like burnt mice.) According to Plutarch, "her actual beauty, it is said, was not in itself so remarkable that none could be compared with her, but the contact of her presence . . . was irresistible; the attraction of her person, joining with the charm of her conversation, and the character that attended all she said or did, was something bewitching. It was a pleasure merely to hear the sound of her voice, with which, like an instrument of many strings, she could pass from one language to another. . . ."

He sounds half in love with her himself.

Whatever she looked like, she bowled Caesar over, and when his reinforcements came he squelched the rebellious Egyptian army for her. In the process he had to burn his own ships and the fire spread and took out part of Alexandria's library. Most of what had been learned up to the time – Shaw called it "the memory of mankind" – went up in smoke and the world had to start over from scratch, but Cleopatra got Egypt back.

When the smoke cleared they found Ptolemy XIII drowned in the Nile in a full suit of golden armor, but as far as we know, his sister hadn't pushed him. Caesar then married her to her youngest brother, Ptolemy XIV, age twelve, but this one didn't have a Pothinus on his side and she ignored him.

When Caesar left, she was pregnant. Anti-Cleopatrans scoff at the notion that Caesar was the father, since he never admitted it himself, but there was plenty he never admitted, including his whole Egyptian fling, and somehow it seems likely. Giving the childless Caesar a son was a much shrewder move than getting pregnant by your twelve-year-old brother and might have done wonders for

Egypt. She named him Ptolemy Caesar, always referred to him as Caesarion, and took him to Rome in 46 B.C. Mindful of her father's mistake, she took Ptolemy XIV, too, to keep an eye on him.

She stayed in Rome as Caesar's guest. They gave fabulous parties and he put up a golden statue of her in the temple of Venus Genetrix, causing a scandal that made him more vulnerable to the people who were plotting to kill him, as they did in March of 44. After he got stabbed, it turned out that he hadn't named Caesarion as his heir, but his great-nephew Octavius, so Cleopatra had to pack up and go home.

By September, Ptolemy XIV was dead. Considerable gossip surrounds his untimely end. All we know is that Cleopatra took a keen interest in pharmaceuticals, and her brother was growing up and might have been more threat than helpmeet. She appointed the toddler Caesarion as co-ruler.

Here the record loses interest in her for several years, between lovers, but she must have been busy. She'd inherited a country plagued by civil wars, Caesar and the Flute Player had drained the coffers, Egypt was broke, and twice more the Nile floods misfired. Somehow, though, by the time the West noticed her again, peace reigned even in fractious Alexandria, she'd played her cards deftly with Rome, and her subjects loved her. According to the first-century A.D. Jewish historian Josephus, she'd negotiated a honey of a deal with the Arabs over some oil rights, and in general managed the economy so well that Egypt was the richest state in the eastern Mediterranean. So rich that

Mark Antony came knocking for funds in 41 B.C. so he could attack the Parthians.

The Romans were still pigheadedly pursuing the triumvirate notion, this time with Octavius, Lepidus, and Antony. If you believe Plutarch, Antony was a simple fellow, generous and easygoing, though a bit of a slob. Cicero says his orgies made him "odious," and there's a story that, after an all-night party, he had a speaking engagement, rose to address the populace, and threw up, while a friend held his gown back so it wouldn't get splattered. Still, he was doing all right until Cleopatra came along and he was, as Dryden laments, "Unbent, unsinewed, made a woman's toy."

Plutarch's description of their meeting on her barge makes poets and movie producers salivate. Who could resist those silver oars and purple sails, those flutes and harps, the wafting perfumes, the costumed maidens, and the queen herself dressed as Venus under a canopy of gold? Not Antony, certainly.

She knew what he'd come for and planned to drive a hard bargain. After a night of love, they sat down to deal: she would pay for his Parthian campaign, he would help fight her enemies and, for good measure, kill Arsinoe, her last sibling. Arsinoe was in Ephesus calling herself queen of Egypt, and Cleopatra took no chances where her family was concerned.

All six of the Flute Player's children seem to have been ambitious and clever. Geneticists tell us not to marry our brothers and sisters, but after three centuries of it the Ptole-

mies could still spawn an energetic brood. Perhaps the geneticists are wrong.

Antony came for money and stayed to play. A sound
relationship with Rome was tops on the whole world's
agenda at the time. The perfect hostess, Cleopatra lowered
her standards of decorum and encouraged her guest in
rowdy revels that have shocked the ages. The ages feel that
all that frivoling means she was a frivolous woman, and
not that, like any Washington lobbyist with a pocketful of
Redskins tickets, she was putting her time and money
where they mattered most.

She drank and gambled and hunted and fished with him.
Sometimes they dressed as servants and roamed the town
teasing the natives. Plutarch's grandfather knew a man
who knew one of her cooks and reported that gargantuan
banquets were prepared but, since they had to be served
fresh, if Antony wanted another round of drinks before
dinner the first banquet was thrown out and a new one
cooked, and so on around the clock. Anyone standing outside the kitchen door must have been half buried in delicacies.

Back in Rome, Antony's third wife, Fulvia, had raised an
army against Octavius, triumvir number two. (Lepidus,
like Crassus, had fizzled out early.) She got whipped, and
Antony had to bid the fleshpots farewell and go patch
things up politically. Fulvia conveniently died and he sealed
the peace by marrying Octavius's sister, Octavia.

Within weeks of the ceremony Cleopatra had twins, Alexander Helios and Cleopatra Selene.

At the news of Antony's marriage Shakespeare's queen

has hysterics and tries to stab the messenger, but Shakespeare's guessing. The real queen probably took it in stride. She knew politics when she saw it, and she had Antony's alliance and a son to cement it and a country to run besides.

No one suggests she had a prime minister, and after Pothinus, who would risk having one? But no one denies the kingdom was in apple-pie order. So there sits our drunken harlot, with Caesarion and the twins in bed, working late by oil-light, signing papyri, meeting with advisors, balancing the budget, approving plans for aqueducts. Adjusting taxes. Administering the free health-care plan, distributing free grain during hard times. Receiving ambassadors and haggling over trade agreements. She might hardly have had time to put eyeliner on, let alone loll in asses' milk, and apparently she slept alone.

Antony finally got it together enough to invade Parthia and once again needed help. He sent for Cleopatra to meet him at Antioch and bring the children. Some see this as strictly business, but Plutarch insists his passion had "gathered strength again, and broke out into a flame." Anyway, they were rapturously reunited, and in the morning she agreed to build him a Mediterranean fleet and feed his army in exchange for most of what's now Lebanon, Syria, Jordan, and southern Turkey. One of her new territories was full of dates and balsam and she promptly leased it back to the resident king, bringing in effortless revenues. Apparently history's most famous lovers spent more time at the bargaining table than in bed.

Did she really love him, or was it pure ambition? Ambition certainly didn't hurt, but it seems she was fond of him, though he probably snored after heavy parties. Sources say she tried to introduce him to the finer things in life and dragged him to learned discussions, which sounds at least affectionate. Maybe they both had a talent for loving useful people; maybe it's not uncommon.

After a happy winter in Antioch, he went off to attack Parthia and she was pregnant again.

The Parthian campaign was a disaster and he lost nearly half his men.

For Cleopatra it was another boy, Ptolemy Philadelphus, and when she'd recovered she went to Antony's rescue with pay and warm clothes for the survivors. Presently Octavia announced that she too was coming to bring supplies. Antony told her to forget it and stay home. As a career move, this was a gamble. Octavius felt his sister had been dissed and told the Romans Antony had deserted them, thrown in his lot with Egypt, and planned to rule the whole East jointly with its queen.

You could see it that way. In a public ceremony in Alexandria he assembled the children, dressed to the teeth and sitting on thrones, and proclaimed Cleopatra Queen of Kings and Caesarion King of Kings. He made his own three offspring royalty, too, and gave them considerable realms that weren't, strictly speaking, his to give. Worst of all, he announced that Caesarion, not Octavius, was Caesar's real son and the real heir to Rome.

Then he divorced Octavia.

All hands prepared for war. Octavius had trouble collecting taxes to pay an army, even after explaining that he was fighting the evil foreigner, not poor deluded Antony. If the lovers had been quick off the mark, they might have invaded Italy at once and won, but instead they retired to Greece to assemble their forces, including Cleopatra's fleet.

Antony would have been better off without a fleet, being more the terra-firma type, but it was Cleopatra's contribution and had cost her a bundle. She insisted on sailing with it, too; her national treasure was stowed in the flagship. They spread their forces around western Greece, where one by one they got picked off by the Romans until our rebels were bottled up at Actium, facing Octavius across the gulf of Ambracia.

Describing battles is best left to the professionals, and besides, the Battle of Actium's rather a mystery. The accepted version is that, while the fight hung in the balance, Cleopatra took her ships and left, either because, being a woman, she was a coward, or because, being treacherous, she'd already sold her lover to Octavius. The besotted Antony, we're told, followed her like a dog and the fight turned into a rout.

With battles, the winner gets to tell the tale. All we really know is that it was a bloody mess and, for whatever reason, Cleopatra managed to retreat with the treasure still intact, enough to build another fleet with change left over.

On land, a lot of Antony's army surrendered, plunging him into sulky uselessness. Cleopatra sent Caesarion away and had her ships dragged by hand across the desert to the Red Sea so she could leave by the back way. Unfortunately the Arabs burned them and she was stranded, but at least she still had money. Octavius wanted money to pay his troops. She wanted Egypt for her children. Deals could be made. Antony even suggested killing himself in trade for Cleopatra's life, but Octavius was bound for Egypt and wouldn't deal. Thus threatened, the queen built a two-storey mausoleum and stuffed it with treasure, along with fuel enough to burn it down if all else failed, and then locked herself into it with her serving maids.

It's unclear whether Antony just assumed she was dead or, from either treachery or pure wickedness, she sent to tell him she was, or whether he was just depressed, but anyway he disemboweled himself. He botched the job – it's harder than you'd think – and lingered long enough to be hauled to the mausoleum and hoisted through the upstairs window, where presumably he died in Cleopatra's arms.

Octavius marched victorious into town. He sent his henchmen to the queen and they tricked their way in, snatched away her dagger, and took her – and her treasure – prisoner.

According to Plutarch, at thirty-nine "her old charm, and the boldness of her youthful beauty had not wholly left her and, in spite of her present condition, still sparkled from within." It didn't help.

She seems to have hated the idea of being dragged through the streets of Rome as a prisoner, as who wouldn't? So she and her ladies dressed up in their best finery and killed themselves.

Octavius did the handsome thing and had her buried with Antony. Then he tracked down and killed Caesarion and annexed Egypt as his own personal colony. The twins and Ptolemy Philadelphus were allowed to live, as long as they kept quiet about it.

The best-remembered Cleo story is the asp smuggled in with the basket of figs. Plutarch, who saw the medical record, mentions it as a rumor, wrestles with the evidence, and concludes that "what really took place is known to no one, since it was also said that she carried poison in a hollow bodkin . . . yet there was not so much as a spot found, or any symptom of poison upon her body, nor was the asp seen within the monument. . . ."

Later it was suggested – probably by Octavius – that she'd tested various substances on her slaves and opted for the asp, but in truth its bite is even less fun than disemboweling and the effects are just as visible. The cobra is offered as a pleasanter alternative, but a cobra with juice enough to kill three adults at a single sitting would have to be six feet long and need a whopping great basket of figs to hide in. And where did it go? Did the dying women chase it around and wrestle it into submission and heave it out the window? Why, when its next victim would certainly be Roman?

Some claimed there were two faint marks on her arm, but they sound like mosquito bites to me. Others insist they saw something like a snake's trail on the sand outside; fat chance, with all those guards and soldiers and distressed citizens milling around shouting and trampling the evidence.

It looks likelier that she'd brewed up a little something to keep handy. She was clever that way; remember the second brother. Octavius's men had patted her down – "shook out her dress," Plutarch says – but she was smarter than they were. And why gamble on the availability of snakes and smugglers when you could bring your own stuff in your suitcase?

When Octavius led his Triumph through Rome, lacking the actual queen he paraded an effigy and pictures of her wreathed in snakes, and the asp theory slithered into history. Maybe he'd heard the rumor and believed it, but it seems probable he started it himself. It would have played well in Rome. In Egypt, the snake was a symbol of royalty and pet of the goddess Isis, but in Rome it was strictly a reptile, and a slimy, sinister way to die, so typical of those Easterners, compared to a forthright Roman whacking out his innards. Being phallic too, it reinforced his other stories about her.

History has always mixed itself with politics and advertising, and in all three arts the best story always carries the day. But why did the man who was now overlord of the universe, undisputed ruler of the Mediterranean world, bother to work so hard to ruin a dead lady's reputation? Maybe she'd been more formidable than any of our surviving stories tell.

We do know she was the last great power of the Hellenistic world, "sovereign queen of many nations," and the last major threat to Rome for a long time. And maybe she overplayed her hand but she never played for nickels and dimes. She might have ruled half the world or even, through her children, the whole thing, and brought the Golden Age of peace she said she was sent to bring. And as Pascal suggested, under a less manly tradition than Rome's a number of things, like Christianity, might have turned out otherwise.

At least she would have left us her own version of who she was, and maybe it would be closer to truth than the others. And then again, given the human urge to tell good stories, maybe not.

Robin Hood
All-American Hero

Robin Hood is the all-American English folk hero, and it's time we brought him over and made him a citizen. The Brits can keep King Arthur, favored legend of their upper classes; hard to imagine American children playing Round Table knights, competing with each other in chastity and nobility while seeking the Holy Grail. But Robin has always been one of us. He serves up all the American virtues as we like to see them – he's independent, outspoken, fearless, individualistic, democratic, generous, humorous, contemptuous of authority, and an unbeatable athlete.

Like us, he thumbs his nose at the king of England.

> And always went good Robin
> By hideout and by hill
> And always slew the king's deer
> And dealt with them at his will

they sang around 1500, nearly three hundred years before we dealt with the king's colonies at *our* will.

Like us, he moves into the woods – Sherwood for him, the new continent or the western frontier for us – and lives off the land. Like us, he creates an egalitarian society there, where friars and yokels eat from the same stew pot.

And like us, he started out a yeoman, however Hollywood may knight him. A yeoman stood above the oppressed mass of laborers but below a "gentleman," who had claims to birth and breeding and stood below a squire, who stood below a knight. Descendants of yeomen populated the American colonies, having enough substance and confidence to make the trip but little to lose by leaving home.

The earliest Robin stories were the simple adventures of a merry, prankish outlaw preying on travelers – often greedy clergymen – on the Great North Road. These "talkyngs" were spread by minstrels among a rough, uneducated audience in the fourteenth and fifteenth centuries; by the sixteenth they were turning up in print and in plays.

Possible dates for a historical Robin range from 1193 to 1320. A historian in the 1440s sets him in 1266, saying "Then arose the famous murderer, Robin Hood, as well as Little John, together with their accomplices among the dispossessed, whom the foolish populace are so inordinately fond of celebrating both in tragedy and comedy." It would be a shame if he were right, since by 1266 Richard the Lion-Hearted had been dead for sixty-six years and his brother John for fifty. This knocks a gaping hole in the movies, which have Robin loyal to swashbuckling Richard, sometimes going with him on Crusades, and rebellious against the traitor John.

Alas, the only king mentioned in the early tales is Edward, probably Edward II passing through Sherwood in 1323. This is chronologically late and cinematically dismal; Edward was a world-class wimp. Best just to ignore history entirely and go along with Errol Flynn and Kevin Costner and Sean Connery and Walt Disney and the rest: Richard I and John have wedged themselves too firmly in our minds with Robin. Besides, they provide the plot. The original Robin stories were born before plots were invented, and a movie needs *something* to hold it together.

Over his six hundred years Robin has changed a lot, adapting himself to different audiences. By the sixteenth century his stories were incorporated into the dances and plays of the May Games, and the Queen of the May got the role of Maid Marian, a new character based on a shepherdess in a French play.

Now that Robin was theater instead of recited verse, audiences began demanding nobility – it made the costumes more exciting. In 1598 an Anthony Munday wrote two plays setting Robin in King Richard's reign and elevating the yeoman rogue to Robert, Earl of Huntington, done out of his inheritance through treachery. (Nobody *ever* got the best of Robin except by treachery.) Munday's earldom followed Robin through the centuries, enthusiastically seconded by the movies (Technicolor likes nobility too).

As his social status rose, so did his ethics. No longer a simple poacher and highwayman, he developed the pureminded ideals we've inherited. The sixteenth-century historian John Major wrote approvingly, "He permitted no harm to women, nor seized the goods of the poor, but helped them generously with what he took from abbots."

Unlikely as it sounds, this became our basic definition of Robin. It gives him his "G" rating; to steal from the rich for fun, as he did originally, sets a bad example for the children. As time went by, we even came to believe that he stole from the rich *in order* to give to the poor, a stretch that could dislocate the broadest imagination. Still, it's likely he was decent enough to the local peasantry. It would have been a sensible precaution for an outlaw.

Maid Marian, Robin's girl, has suffered gentrification in Hollywood's hands. In the classic 1938 Errol Flynn epic, she's played by Olivia de Havilland, and de Havilland is every inch a lady; who can imagine her living under a tree with a passel of pickpockets? Marian became a noble Norman with royal connections who lives in a castle and wrings her hands a lot. This is nice for the costume-designers, but as a character she lacks the clout she started with.

Early Marians were no wimps. The one in an ancient ballad goes out looking for Robin in the forest, dressed as a pageboy, and when she meets him, fights him for an hour before recognizing his voice. In a 1598 play, she's Matilda Fitz Walter, who escapes from the lechery of evil King John and follows her lover to Sherwood Forest, where they change their names to Marian and Robin. Perhaps the most satisfying heroine for American tastes is in T. H. White's *The Sword in the Stone*, a merry lass living under the greenwood tree, wearing a green smock and a quiverful of arrows and commanding the menfolk in battle. As skilled in woodcraft and archery as the others, she goes along on even the most dangerous adventures. She's brave, kind, resourceful, and suntanned, and entirely suitable for transatlantic transplant.

As time passed, Robin the once-lighthearted outlaw got saddled with more and more virtuous responsibility. In 1795 Joseph Ritson makes him a social rebel, nobly opposing tyranny. Sir Walter Scott's *Ivanhoe,* in 1820, makes him a Saxon chafing under the Norman occupation, though by Robin's time the Norman/Saxon conflict was a thoroughly dead issue. And the 1991 *Prince of Thieves* has him leading a band of tax protesters in a kind of woodsy early Boston Tea Party.

Historians rage at this tinkering with the original tales, but the truth is, the original tales were no great loss. Few ever turn up in the movies, and small wonder. Robin meets a fat abbot, tricks or fights him, and takes his bags of gold. Or lures him into Sherwood, feasts him lavishly, and *then* takes his bags of gold. Robin goes forth in disguise, or several disguises, in search of adventure. When he needs his men he blows three blasts on his bugle horn. He meets a stout fellow on the road, challenges him to combat, gets soundly bested, laughs and invites him to join up; the fellow always joins. The sheriff of Nottingham lures Robin to an archery contest, which Robin always wins, then tries to capture him. Little John shoots the sheriff in the rump. In the end Robin is taken by treachery and, just before he dies, shoots an arrow through a window; its landing spot will be his grave. Simple, repetitive stuff.

The magic isn't in the stories. Maybe it never was. It's in the very thought of Robin, carefree, wicked Robin (looking much like Errol Flynn) surrounded by his loyal men, feasting on ale and venison, jesting and singing in his forest, laughing at the law, like a more convivial Huck Finn. Like a lazier Daniel Boone, a luckier Davy Crockett, a merrier Jesse James.

He can't be happy nowadays in Sherwood, Sherwood shriveled to a theme park, its great trees long since sacrificed to the British Navy. Not after living under the greenwood oak, a landmark tree with room for two hundred men to eat and sleep under its arms. As John Keats observed,

> And if Marian should have
> Once again her forest days,
> She would weep, and he would craze;
> He would swear, for all his oaks,
> Fall'n beneath the dockyard strokes,
> Have rotted on the briny seas;
> She would weep that her wild bees
> Sang not to her – strange! that honey
> Can't be got without hard money!

We in America still have woods in Maine, forests in the northwest, honey for Marian. The Robin legend has suffered stranger changes than a simple trip across the seas; let's bring him here where he belongs. He can tease the Park Service for entertainment. Protect spotted owls instead of Saxons. And maybe shake down an occasional tourist caught littering the pathway and relieve him of his bags of gold.

POCAHONTAS
Princess Between Two Worlds

". . . AND JUST AS THE savages were about to chop off John Smith's head, the beautiful Indian princess threw herself upon him, defying her father, and saved his life."

Then what? Well, she married somebody else. Generations of schoolchildren are disgusted: what kind of a story is that? Why didn't the ungrateful toad marry her?

Sorry, children. American history is short on heroines. We rummage in the past to find something for little girls, a change from young Abe doing his homework by firelight and young George with his cherry tree, and what do we find? Betsy Ross, a seamstress who was paid to sew a flag from a new pattern, and did. Hardly a tale to set the heart racing. And Pocahontas, who apparently fell in love with one Englishman and married another.

The real Pocahontas story is more interesting, but we can't tell the children because it shows our earliest settlers in a dim light. Heroic princesses are strictly optional; heroic settlers are basic education.

Perhaps "settlers" is the wrong word. It sounds like

hardy, self-reliant folk come to build houses and plow fields to make a better life. The Englishmen who landed in tidewater Virginia in the spring of 1607 were a lazy bunch of renegades, sent by the Virginia Company purely for profit. John Smith himself called them "the scumme of the world." They came for gold, and they didn't plan to dig for it either; surely the simpleminded Indians would just hand it to them in exchange for trinkets, and then show them the trade route to the Orient through this inconvenient chunk of land.

Powhatan, Pocahontas's father, wasn't quite the childlike savage they had in mind. He was a proud and subtle man, overlord of the thirty-some tribes – perhaps 9,000 people living in 160 villages – who prospered on fishing and agriculture around the lower Chesapeake. And the new arrivals on the *Susan Constant,* the *Godspeed,* and the *Discovery* weren't the first "clothed people" he'd heard of. Recently a shipful of Europeans had stopped by and repaid the hospitality of Powhatan's Rappahannocks by murdering their king.

The adventurers were greeted with skirmishes. Captain Christopher Newport sailed his ships up the Powhatan River (now the James) to a swampy isthmus they christened Jamestown. (It was on the hunting grounds of Powhatan's Paspaheghs, but nobody asked.) In May, an Indian attack killed and injured a bunch of men and boys, so by June the English managed to finish a crude sort of fort.

Between hostilities they traded with the Indians, though not for gold. Pocahontas came to visit. William Strachey wrote that she was "well-featured but wanton . . . of the age then of 11 or 12 years" and would "gett the boyes forth with her into the markett place and make them wheele, falling on their hands turning their heeles upwardes, whome she would follow, and wheele her self naked as she was all the Fort over."

"Pocahontas" was a nickname meaning mischievous and merry. Her real name was Matoaka, or "Little Snow Feather"; this may have seemed more appropriate when she was younger. She was Powhatan's favorite among his thirty children and plainly spoiled and spirited. Powhatan himself sent an occasional emissary but didn't lower himself to visit; no doubt he was getting reports on the English from his daughter.

On June 22, Captain Newport and two of the ships went back to England, leaving Edward Wingfield in charge of the 104 people inside the fort and Captain John Smith in charge outside.

They had the long Chesapeake summer to work in, but nobody did any planting, fishing, or hunting, partly because of Indian snipers in the long grass outside the fort. (Later a friendly Indian suggested that they cut the grass. It hadn't occurred to them.)

At harvest time they traded for food with the Indians, but by December all except forty were dead, most of starvation, though dysentery, typhoid, and drinking saltwater took their toll. Smith went up the Chickahominy to trade for supplies and try to meet Powhatan and ask about that route to the Orient.

He fell afoul of some of Powhatan's deerhunters, killed

two, and retreated but got hopelessly mired in a bog and captured. The leader, a brother of Powhatan's, took him on a tour of the tribes, showing him to the Rappahannocks, who were still simmering over the murder of their king. Happily, Smith was a short man and the captain who'd done the deed was remembered as tall.

Finally Smith was taken to Werowocomoco, Powhatan's headquarters on what is now the York River, and delivered to the great chief and his entourage, including Pocahontas.

In his "Generall Historie," Smith tells us that Powhatan's people "feasted him after their best barbarous manner," and after dinner hauled in two great stones. Then, he wrote, "as many as could layd hands on him, dragged him to them, and thereon laid his head, and being ready with their clubs, to beate out his braines, Pocahontas the Kings dearest daughter, when no intreaty could prevale, got his head in her armes, and laid her owne upon his to save him from death." Elsewhere he adds, "at the minute of my execution, she hazarded the beating out of her owne braines to save mine."

Anyway, that's the way Smith saw it, and the way the legend grew. Smith was no anthropologist, and he must have been badly frightened. Two days later the Indians took him to a house in the woods, where Powhatan came to explain that, in token of their friendship, Smith was to go back to Jamestown and send him "two great gunnes, and a gryndstone." In return, Powhatan would give him "the Country of Capahowosick, and for ever esteeme him as his sonne Nantaquod."

Odd indeed, from a man who had ordered his brains

beaten out. Most modern historians believe that Smith's alarming experience was actually an adoption ceremony. At this point Powhatan had no reason to kill Smith and good reasons not to; he was not a violent man, and the English had things he wanted. However, a great chief cannot wheedle. The adopting father must first show his new son who's boss, who has power of life and death around here. To keep his own dignity, he apparently appointed Pocahontas adoptive sister, or sponsor, to the new member of the family. Her rescue symbolized her role.

There's also the disquieting possibility that the whole rescue story was pure invention. Smith never mentioned it to anyone until he wrote the "Generall Historie," years after Pocahontas was dead, and it seems odd that such an accomplished public relations man, who so enjoyed burnishing his own adventures, would keep such a rattling good yarn under wraps for so long. It would be a pity not to believe it, though, short as we are on heroines.

Whatever happened, Pocahontas did feel responsible for the lazy, helpless little band. In the hard times to come, she acted as her father's ambassador and the colony's benefactor. When her father grew mistrustful of the English, she did indeed risk her life by helping them behind his back.

Powhatan sent Smith back to Jamestown with a dozen guards to fetch the promised cannon and grindstone. Unfortunately, they were too heavy to drag away.

In London, the Virginia Company scolded Captain Newport for bringing "gold" that was only worthless rocks and sent him back for better booty. Five days after his return with relief supplies, Jamestown burned. All but three small buildings were gone, including the storehouse with the food.

Powhatan sent help. Smith wrote, "Had the Salvages not fed us, we had directly starved. . . . And this relief . . . was commonly brought us by this Lady Pocahontas." He added later that she "not only for feature, countenance, and proportion much exceedeth any of the rest of [Powhatan's] people, but for wit, and spirit, the only Nonpareil of his Country."

Newport went back to England again. Spring planting time came, but the English had all quit doing anything but scratching around for what Smith called "gilded dirt."

In the summer, Newport returned with seventy-eight new settlers. He had forgotten to bring any food for the winter, but he did bring orders from the Company that, to cement his cooperation, Powhatan was to be brought to Jamestown and crowned "emperor."

Powhatan was not as honored as the Company expected. He replied, "If your king has sent me presents, I also am a king and this is my land. . . . Your father [he meant Captain Newport] is to come to me, not I to him, nor yet to your fort." So the English dragged his presents, including a large bed and a copper crown, up the river. Powhatan was unimpressed, and refused to kneel to be crowned. For gifts in return, he gave them the deerskin cloak he was wearing, a pair of used moccasins, and some corn.

There were now some two hundred English squatters on his land; they were disrespectful; they showed no sign of leaving; and they couldn't even feed themselves. He told Pocahontas to stay away from Jamestown.

She didn't. Rebellious or curious, she "freely frequented" the fort, accompanied by her "wilde traine," bringing supplies.

In January of 1609, Powhatan invited Smith to visit, promising him a boatload of corn in exchange for various items – that grindstone he still wanted, a rooster, a hen, and guns.

Smith had ruled that no guns were to be traded with the Indians, but guns were Powhatan's weak point. He didn't know how to use them but he loved their aura of power. He was disappointed.

His meeting with Smith was ominous. He said, "Captain Smith, many do inform me, your coming hither is not for trade, but to invade my people, and possess my country." The cold shadow of the future had touched him.

That evening, Pocahontas came secretly to Smith "through the irksome woods" and warned him that her father planned to have him killed, this time in earnest. Smith offered her some trinkets in return for her help but she refused them, saying that her father would kill her if he caught her with English gifts.

As in the well-built Greek tragedy, the possibilities of a happy ending for father and daughter, settler and native, were dwindling.

Under Pocahontas's direction Smith eluded the plot and returned to Jamestown, where he found himself in full charge, the other council members having drowned when their boat turned over. He was an unpopular leader, making the men work if they expected to eat. Conditions might have improved, though, except for an accident with an exploding powder bag that severely injured his thigh and called for civilized medical help.

At the same time three hundred new settlers arrived, bearing word of a new governor, Lord De La Warre, coming to replace Smith. And by now the Indians had decided that if they got rid of Smith, the rest of the English would leave, and kept trying to kill him. So did some of his disgruntled comrades.

He went back to England, leaving Virginia without its only really sensible man. The Indians, encouraged, redoubled their raids.

Pocahontas came no more and the winter of 1609–1610 was called "the Starving Time." The colonists ate the horses first, then "doggs Catts Ratts and myce," followed by boots and shoes, then serpents and roots from the woods. One fellow was said to have killed his wife and salted her down for his larder. Smith left five hundred settlers in September; by spring there were only sixty.

The colonists had guns and ammunition, the woods were full of game, the rivers so thick with fish that Smith mentions scooping them up in a pan. With such abundance, it's hard to imagine people there eating their shoes and loved ones, but no doubt there were reasons.

In June they prepared to abandon the colony, but just as they set sail, rescue came with a shipload of new settlers, the new governor, and a year's supply of food.

Indian troubles, however, escalated. De La Warre ordered all captured guns and prisoners returned; Powhatan refused. Blood was shed. Ill and unhappy, the governor returned to England and was replaced by the fierce Sir Thomas Dale, who felt extermination was the only answer to the Indian problem. He'd brought armor with him and, their arrows now useless, the Indians fell back on magic charms.

In 1613 Pocahontas, on a trade mission for her father, heard of a ship from Jamestown, Captain Samuel Argall commanding, anchored nearby. Unable to resist, she went to visit. Argall lured her aboard by treachery and took her prisoner, hoping to ransom some English hostages and stolen guns.

Powhatan balked at the demands. Pocahontas was sent to the Rocke Hall parsonage, near Henrico, where she was subjected to religious instruction, tight English clothes, and proper shoes. After some skirmishing, Powhatan returned the prisoners but only some broken guns, saying that the rest would be forthcoming when he saw his daughter. The English refused.

Time passed. Pocahontas must have been bitterly hurt. She said "that if her father had loved her, he would not value her lesse than olde swords, peeces, or axes: wherefore she would stil dwel with the English men, who loved her."

The widower John Rolfe, a pious tobacco planter, had taken over her Christian education with zeal. How she felt about him is not recorded, but her rage and grief over her father's rejection surely helped Rolfe's suit.

Rolfe himself deplored her barbarous background, but decided it was God's will that he save her by marrying her. He wrote Governor Dale for permission, "for the good of this plantation, for the honour of our countrie, for the glory of God, for my owne salvacion, and for the converting to the true knowledge of God and Jesus Christ, an unbeleeving creature."

Dale agreed, and Pocahontas was duly baptized, renamed "Rebecca," and in April 1614, married.

Her father had vowed never to put himself into English hands, but he sent some relatives as witnesses. In honor of the marriage, he declared a kind of sorrowful truce, known in the colony as the Peace of Pocahontas. He said that too many people had been killed, "which by my occasion ther shall never bee more . . . for I am now olde, and would gladly end my daies in peace . . . my country is large enough, I will remove my selfe farther from you." Sad words from so proud a man.

In late 1614 or early 1615, the Rolfes had a son and called him Thomas.

Meanwhile, back in London, the Virginia experiment was under fire. Rolfe's tobacco scheme would become the great cash cow, but nobody knew that yet. Angry messages asked why the colony had failed to produce as expected, not just gold, but pineapples, oranges, silkworms, and wine. Support dried up.

In a public relations ploy to encourage investment, Governor Dale took Pocahontas, the baby, assorted relatives, and Rolfe to London in the spring of 1616.

Some treated the princess as a joke, some were impressed. Smith said his friends admitted "they have seene many English Ladies worse favored, proportioned and behavioured." Strangely, she and Smith didn't meet until she'd been some months in England. When they did, she reproached him with neglect and turned her back on him.

He did his best for her socially, and wrote Queen Anne, "two or three yeeres, she next under God, was still the instrument to preserve this Colonie from death, famine and utter confusion." She was invited to a masque and some entertainments at court, and introduced to her own future in Virginia, where she was to be held responsible for the peace and the conversion of the Indians to Christianity and English ways.

Simon van de Passe made an engraving of her. By the standards of her day, she looks sharp-featured, almost witchlike, but with huge, wary, intelligent eyes. The engraving gives her age as twenty-one (no one knows for sure) but she looks much older. She was ill.

The winter of 1617 was mild but deadly damp, the air in London was infamous, and most of the Indian visitors fell ill with coughs and what was called consumption.

The baby and his nurses were ill, too, but Rolfe was impatient to get back to his tobacco and made plans to depart. When the ship was at Gravesend and about to sail, Pocahontas's condition worsened until even Rolfe noticed, and she was taken ashore, where she died at an inn.

"All men must die," she said to Rolfe.

Her heart must have been heavy. Probably she didn't relish the impossible task of turning her kin into docile Englishmen. Certainly her once-doting father had treated her shabbily. Perhaps she had loved Smith – she risked enough for him – and he had ignored her. She loved her son, but he would survive. Perhaps she wasn't sorry to die, the once-wild princess coughing her lungs out in a gray country, so far from the Chesapeake lands where she'd been welcomed in every village as Powhatan's dearest child.

Little Thomas, too ill to travel, stayed behind, to be raised by a merchant uncle. Back in Jamestown, the peace collapsed. In one bloody assault Powhatan's successor killed 350 colonists. Kept afloat by the burgeoning tobacco trade, however, Virginia survived.

Thomas Rolfe never saw his father again, but he went back to Virginia in 1635, where he married and had a daughter, Jane. Jane was to have many descendants, including Woodrow Wilson's wife Edith, but her ancestors, the Virginia Indians, had been almost entirely destroyed and supplanted, as Powhatan had foretold.

In 1699 the capital moved to Williamsburg and Jamestown declined and was eventually abandoned. By 1890, where America's first permanent English colony was planted, only part of a church from 1639 and traces of a churchyard remained.

Its real monument, though, will always be the story of its headstrong princess, caught in the crush between two irreconcilable worlds.

WILLIAM PENN

The Man Who Owned a Country

IN CELEBRATION OF WILLIAM PENN'S 350th birthday in
1994, Philadelphia's Historical Society of Pennsylvania put
together an exhibit from his colony's early days. Among
the odds and ends was Penn's 1681 advertisement for settlers, beginning "Since (by the good providence of God) a
Country in America is fallen to my lot . . ."

Not everyone gets to write a line like that. Not everyone
gets his own country – forty-five thousand square miles to
arrange and bestow and govern, a country of rivers and
forests and fat farmland. William Penn, Proprietor, was
answerable only to the King of England, and paid, as rent,
two beaver skins, delivered to Windsor Castle on the first
of January every year. Those of us who have bought even
an eighth of a suburban acre and gazed on its possibilities
with awe may pause to consider the pleasure of Mr. Penn,
with a Country fallen to his lot. Fallen by the good providence of – in addition to God – his father's great friend
Charles II.

Not that Penn was a stranger to landowning. He'd inherited thousands of acres in Ireland and England and

married into more. But that was the Old World, with its laws and customs and prejudices already in place, the Old World that jailed those who, like Penn, subscribed to unofficial religions. The New World was new, waiting for Penn's shaping hands to people it and design its government and future. Perhaps, in the privacy of his study, he tossed his curly wig in the air and kicked up his buckled shoes and danced; seventeenth-century Quakers were much less sober and decorous than their descendants.

A different man, or a man with different children, would have left his marks all over the mid-Atlantic. We'd have ducal manors with thousand-acre lawns belonging to sixteen generations of Penns and pay five dollars to visit their gardens in spring. But Penn didn't take root in his country. Perhaps for him it seemed more a concept than a home. He left us various legacies – Philadelphia, for instance, and a pluralistic society, and an appreciation of trade and commerce – but Penn, the man, slipped away.

We don't even know for certain what he looked like.

We can go to Pennsbury Manor, on forty-three acres reclaimed from an original eighty-four hundred, and visit the spot where Penn once lived on a bend of the Delaware River, twenty- six miles north of Philadelphia. He already owned the land under the terms of the Charter, but, scrupulous always in his dealings with the Lenni Lenape natives (who'd considered it theirs for twelve thousand years), he insisted on paying for the place. It cost him three hundred fifty fathoms (a fathom was six feet) of wampum, three hundred guilders, twenty white blankets, twenty fathoms of "strawd waters," sixty fathoms of coarse woolen cloth, twenty kettles, twenty guns, twenty coats, forty shirts, forty pairs of stockings, twenty assorted gallons of rum, cider, and beer, and an unspecified quantity of hoes, knives, glasses, shoes, pipes, scissors, combs, and tobacco.

Penn spent some of his time here in the summers from 1699 to 1701, with his second wife, Hannah, daughter Letitia, and infant son, John, born in Philadelphia. He was often downriver, though, in his house in town. He was a great believer in the wholesome country life, especially for children, but he had a colony to supervise, and he was a gregarious man. He commuted back and forth in a barge rowed by six oarsmen; the trip took five hours. In the winters, before the river froze, the family moved into Philadelphia.

In 1701 financial affairs called Penn back to England, and he and his family never saw Pennsbury again. Unused, the house and barns fell to ruin, and in 1792 his descendants sold the land. After that it passed from hand to hand, and by 1929 there was no sign left of Penn's intentions except the old foundations. In 1932 the Charles Warner Company donated the site to the state, and the Pennsylvania Historical Commission began reconstructing the manor, working from archaeological remains and Penn's letters to his builders.

Today, the brick Georgian house facing its highway, the river, is dignified but not overwhelming – Penn's English houses were apparently much grander. A center hall separates the family drawing and dining rooms from Penn's parlor and bedroom. The second floor holds three bedrooms and a nursery, with Hannah's private sitting room opening from her bedroom. Hannah Callowhill Penn was a third-generation Quaker, but she saw nothing impious in a bit of color; her guest room is quite startling with its yellow and scarlet hangings, and the paneling everywhere is painted in warm, strong tones.

Behind the house, the usual outbuildings have been reconstructed and token farm animals installed. One of the geriatric horses is called Tamerlane, in honor of Penn's high-spirited white stallion. The sheep are clipped on the popular Sheep-Shearing Day in spring. A torpid peacock decorates the grounds, and the kitchen gardens are tidily packed with fruit trees, gooseberry bushes, lavender hedges, and herb and vegetable beds. A rooster crows. Three Red Devon cattle with imposing horns regard the visitor, calmly chewing.

Though this isn't Monticello or Mount Vernon, with their sense of the owners' lives inside their walls, as a model of a rich man's country retreat in the late seventeenth century, it has a comfortable, almost familiar charm. But no traces remain of the man himself.

Back in the Historical Society, there's a pair of chalk drawings, a double-chinned Penn and a formidable Hannah, circa 1698; they're considered likely to be authentic. If so, this may be Penn's only likeness, though the "armor portrait" has its supporters. An eighteenth-century copy of a lost original, it shows Penn – if it is he – in armor, presumably during a brief military foray in Ireland. The shoulder-length wig is soft and wavy, the mouth full and sensitive, the eyes huge, dark, and poetic; somehow it doesn't speak to us of the cocky young firebrand Penn.

Philadelphians think of him as Billy, the thirty-seven-foot statue on City Hall, usually seen from far below at the rear. The gull's-eye view of its face is classically, almost absurdly, handsome, but sculptor Alexander Milne Calder was only guessing.

In 1772, ninety years after the event, Benjamin West painted Penn at his famous (though possibly legendary) council with the Indians under the Treaty Elm during his first visit to the colony. West worked from reports of Penn's looks during his second visit, making him strangely middle-aged, but did have him wearing his famous bright-blue silk sash.

The sash, at least, is authentic. It's here in a case at the Historical Society, faded but still wearable. Penn's first wife, Gulielma, made it for him. Here, too, are a cane chair and a massive bun-footed chest, said to be from Pennsbury, and a pine cradle that a descendant of Penn's housekeeper donated, though it looks too cheap for a man who lived as sumptuously as Penn.

Penn was luckily born. His father was a naval hero, later knighted by Charles II, and a man of property. Penn's childhood was divided between a country estate in Essex and a castle in Ireland. At sixteen he went to Christ Church College in Oxford, which was then under the deanly thumb of John Fell, immortalized in the student verse beginning "I do not like thee, Doctor Fell." Determined to replace the last traces of Cromwell's Puritans with the Church of England, Fell made chapel attendance and the wearing of surplices compulsory.

Young Penn didn't like being ordered around. It would

be wrong to call a Founding Father "spoiled," but certainly Sir William was away much of the time when Penn was a boy, and certainly when he came home from the high seas he was the fondest and most forebearing of parents. And certainly young Penn wasn't used to obedience.

He refused to go to chapel. He was rude about student activities, which he called "hellish darkness and debauchery." (During the merry Restoration years, *not* to go drinking and wenching was radical behavior, and Penn was nothing if not radical.) He took to visiting secret worship sessions and outlawed lectures, and in his second year, he managed to get expelled. With his father's high connections at court, it can't have been easy. Judging from his later nose-thumbing at mayors and magistrates, it seems likely Penn made himself thoroughly obnoxious to the authorities.

His disappointed father sent him off to spend a couple of years in France, where he studied under Moise Amyraut, author of *La Morale Chretienne*, an advocate of personal communication with God without bossy supervision by church personnel.

Religion in the seventeenth century was a matter of intense concern to everyone, as central to life as food and far more contentious. Penn's religion apparently didn't show on the surface, however. When he went back to London, the irascible diarist Samuel Pepys wrote that Penn had "a great deal, if not too much, of the vanity of the French garb, and affected manner of speech and gait." Pepys was a mighty snappy dresser himself, and if he found young Penn's clothes vain, they must have been amazing.

Sir William, still determined to secure his son a government post, sent him to law school at Lincoln's Inn, a project interrupted when the plague swept through London. Now crippled with gout, the father next sent Penn to Ireland, to check on his lands and tenantry and collect the rents. Instead our hero fell under the spell of Thomas Loe, an irresistible Quaker speaker. Conversion struck him so suddenly that he rose in the meeting and stood there mutely, tears pouring down his face. He was twenty-two, and he had found his cause.

In the young rebel's eyes, it must have been an extra attraction that his new faith was illegal. Attending Quaker meetings was punishable by fines, imprisonment, banishment and, for those who persisted, slavery. What young man of spirit could resist?

Inevitably Penn was arrested, along with the rest of a meeting. When the mayor saw the young cavalier's elegant finery, he tried to let him go; surely this was no Quaker. But Penn could never resist an argument and delivered such a harangue that he got locked up with the rest. At the jailhouse door he unbuckled his sword and handed it with a flourish to a bystander, announcing that henceforth he would go unarmed. (He had a weakness for grandstanding. This is seldom a drawback in religious leaders.)

Naturally, the well-connected young man was promptly released; naturally, Sir William heard of it and invited him home to explain himself.

Penn faced his father and kept his hat on in the house, as a mark of Quakerly nonrespect, addressing his sire as "thee." "Thee" was the familiar and singular form of "you," like the French "*tu*" instead of "*vous*," and it was the wrong thing to say to your boss, your father, or your king.

Sir William begged his son to promise that he'd at least say "you" when next he met the king and the Duke of York. Penn retorted that the Lord's light shown equally in all men; he was the equal of any king, and he'd call him "thee." Poor Sir William dropped to his gouty knees and prayed to God for his beloved firstborn to be delivered of this madness. Penn opened a casement and threatened to jump out the window if his father didn't stop.

Happily, a visitor interrupted the discussion.

Biographers recount the scene to show us the strength of Penn's conviction and his father's narrow-mindedness. Still, it's hard not to think of those unfortunate parents of the 1960s whose children dropped out of Harvard to go meditate on communes. A religion that didn't just condone being rude to your father but positively required it must have had a certain charm for the young rebels of the day.

Penn now set forth on his chosen career, not as the ambassador of his father's dreams but as a messenger of the Friendly Persuasion, ineligible for any government post because no Quaker will swear an oath of allegiance. Early Quakers were less concerned with modesty and humility than with defiance, and Penn could defy with the best of them. The illegal meetings were held openly, and the jails filled up with Quakers. Penn used his court connections to get them out; they got themselves back in. He himself spent over seven months in the Tower for writing a pamphlet against the Trinity called "The Sandy Foundation Shaken."

In failing health, Sir William needed his son to administer his estates. Penn, though he had no trouble spending the
income, found business details boring and ignored them.
All his life, his distaste for such worldly matters as bills and
accounts would get him into serious trouble; he never both-
ered to read anything before signing it. (In later days, he
was surprised to find he'd mortgaged the entire colony of
Pennsylvania to a man named Ford and couldn't make the
payments. We almost had a "Fordsylvania.")

He preached, got arrested, refused to swear on the Bible,
sassed the judges, went to jail, pulled some royal strings,
wrote furious letters and sixty defiant religious pamphlets,
got released, and drove around in his carriage spreading the
word. He married the lovely Gulielma Springett, who bore
him a multitude of children, losing the usual percentage in
infancy and the most promising, Springett, at twenty-one.
(The number-two son, William Jr., was a total disaster.)

Penn developed a loyal following and, unsurprisingly,
powerful enemies. He still had royal friends, though, and it
might have been to save his neck that Charles II gave him
Pennsylvania in 1681. The king explained the grant to
Penn by saying it discharged an old debt to Sir William, and
to the Privy Council by saying it was a secluded, faraway
place in which to dispose of the troublesome Quakers.

America brought out the best in Penn. As lord of the land,
he no longer needed to bristle at being pushed around;
there was no one to push him. He called his new country
"an holy experiment" and turned over much of his personal power to the people. He designed a Provincial Coun-

cil and a General Assembly to make laws, and arranged a
government ensuring that "the will of one man may not
hinder the good of the whole country."

For the resident Indians he provided the right of trial
before six settlers and six Indians. He wrote them a letter
saying that those who had cheated them in the past made
God angry, and he wanted "to win and gain your love and
friendship by a kind, just and peaceable life." Apparently
he did. They remembered Penn fondly for generations as a
uniquely trustworthy white man.

Under his laws only Christians could hold public office,
but anyone, even Jews, could live in the colony, provided
they believed in "the one Almighty and eternal God." This
irritated some of his fellow Quakers, who had suffered
much from the Church of England and would rather they
stayed home, but Penn insisted that in his colony "no one
was to be molested or prejudiced for their religious persuasion."

He curtailed capital punishment; he reformed the prison
system. He created a just and gentle government, astonishing for its time; Penn had grown into an astonishing man.
In 1683 Francis Daniel Pastorius, an influential early settler, wrote, "William Penn is loved and praised by the
people. Even the old vicious inhabitants must recognize
they have never seen so wise a ruler." The once-hotheaded,
conceited young dandy who couldn't bear authority had
invented a world that tempered authority and prevented
tyranny.

Just as few of us get a country as a gift, few of us get to
plan a city from scratch, and Penn, who had known

crowded London through the Great Plague and the Great Fire, had strong ideas about street layout and the healthiness of open space.

His two main thoroughfares, Broad and Market (originally High) streets, are so wide they seem peaceful even in today's traffic and let in long swaths of sky and daylight that refresh the city soul. Penn declared the spot on the Delaware where he first landed a public dock, and today Penn's Landing still belongs to the public for riverside strolling and summer concerts. Three of the generous, leafy public squares he planned – now called Rittenhouse, Logan, and Washington – still breathe greenery into the city and fill up in summer with sunbathers, lovers, and pigeon-feeders. He donated the land for the Quaker meeting house at Fourth and Arch streets; another gentle oasis, its rosy old bricks absorb anxieties and soften the pace of the days.

And the city's signature Liberty Bell still draws steady streams of visitors, most of whom believe it has something to do with American Independence. Actually, it was cast in London to commemorate the fiftieth anniversary of Penn's 1701 Charter of Government. Its inscription – "Proclaim Liberty throughout all the land" – means Penn's idea of liberty, not Jefferson's.

Best of all, Penn's original town is still the concentrated heart and soul of the modern city, the place to be, with everything within walking distance. In the golden age of nightclubs, Philadelphia was a joke, the town that rolled up its sidewalks at ten, but it was always a pleasure to live in. People can still live and visit here pleasantly, and walk in the shade of street-side trees that grow to imposing size.

William Penn and his Quakers made Philadelphia perhaps the most civilized and amiable of Eastern cities, where pressures rarely reach the boiling point and horns are rarely blown in anger.

Penn left a deep thumbprint on Philadelphia, and on the state. It's sad that he couldn't live here long enough – barely four years in his two visits – to leave us a face as familiar as Franklin's.

Billy, we hardly knew thee.

BETSY ROSS
Did She or Didn't She?

EVERY JUNE 14 YOUR LOCAL newspaper will tell you
that Elizabeth Griscom Ross Ashburn Claypoole, a.k.a.
Betsy Ross, is a myth, and didn't make the first flag any
more than Columbus discovered America. Most people
pay no attention. They go right on leafing through the
paper toward the funnies, and from time to time they take
the children to the Betsy Ross shrine in Philadelphia, because Betsy is our great American heroine, though it's hard
to explain to the kids just what was so heroic about sewing
a flag together. Reupholstering chairs, Betsy's regular line
of work, takes much more heroism than sewing flags. Flags
don't have coil springs to break loose and smack you in
the eye.

In 1968, during a squabble over the whereabouts of
Betsy's body, the *Philadelphia Inquirer* quoted the attorney
for the Betsy Ross House as saying, "Betsy Ross is the most
famous woman in American history. There are probably
more women who identify with Betsy Ross throughout the
United States than any other female figure in our country's

past." You might think we could idolize someone a bit zippier, like Harriet Tubman or Clara Barton, but there's no accounting for taste. Unless, of course, it's a purely masculine taste, and the sweetly sewing Betsy more acceptable than boat-rockers who smuggled slaves and badgered the government for field hospitals.

Woodrow Wilson said the tale of Betsy Ross was "a beautiful legend, would that it were true." Actually, as a legend she's not in the same league with, say, Rip Van Winkle, or even Bigfoot. She was a struggling young widow with an upholstery shop and connections in Congress. Congress wanted a flag, so they took her a design and asked her to whip up a prototype for Congressional approval. She did. She needed the money. Now, if that's a beautiful legend I'm Paul Bunyan and Babe the Blue Ox.

When you ask your local paper who did sew the first flag, it just shrugs. It says there's no evidence that Betsy did it. However, there's no evidence that anyone else did either.

Look at it this way. Once there were no American flags, and now they're floating over every used-car lot and small-town bank in the country. Since they can't all have appeared at once like a hatch of mosquitoes, it stands to reason there was a first one. And if there was, somebody must have made it. If somebody, why not Betsy? The defense rests.

The prosecution's case is that nobody mentioned the matter for nearly a hundred years. The prosecution takes it for granted that she would have been running around Philadelphia bragging about it, being wined and dined by a grateful public and giving out interviews right and left.

They think whole books would have been written about her, and songs composed in her honor. Since there weren't any songs, and Betsy just sat around quietly covering chairs and making more flags for the next fifty years, they say she's a liar and a legend to boot.

Nobody would have heard of her if it hadn't been for her grandson, one William J. Canby. According to him, he was eleven and she was eighty-four and on her deathbed when she told him about it. This was in 1836. He thought it over until 1870, when he read a long pompous paper about it to the Pennsylvania Historical Society. The Historical Society (those who were still awake) greeted it with hoots of derision and didn't even bother to file a copy.

The paper runs to thirty-two closely written pages, and Canby didn't stint on the ruffles and flourishes, like, "Unless we can redeem the past and by a careful re-survey of the acts of our ancestors, as revealed in ancient manuscripts carefully preserved, or in the almost equally well-preserved traditional lore, with which every locality in the old states abounds, discover who were the real actors in the drama, the magnificent fact of its conception is lost forever. . . . We have no allusions here to any other flag than '*The Flag of the United States*.' "

He lumbers up on his prey, and pounces: "We believe the fact is not generally known that to Philadelphia belongs the honor of having first flung the 'Star-Spangled Banner' to the breeze, and that to a Philadelphia lady, long since gone to her fathers, belongs the honor of having made the first flag with her own hands."

I assume you could hear a pin drop as he introduced

his forebear, a Quaker lass, born in 1752 to Rebecca and Samuel Griscom. Wishful to earn her own living she apprenticed herself in an upholstery shop, and presently married a fellow apprentice, John Ross, and they set up in business together. When John died, she found herself a widow at twenty-four, in financial straits and struggling to keep the shop afloat. Canby saith, "She often pondered over the future, and brooded sometimes almost to despondency upon her troubles, yet she always rallied when she reflected upon the goodness of Providence who had never deserted her."

Well, imagine her surprise when George Washington walked in, along with an official delegation of Congressman Robert Morris and one Colonel (some say General) George Ross, aide to Washington, signer of the Declaration of Independence, and uncle of her late husband. They asked her if she could make a flag, and "she said she did not know but she could try."

The prosecution triumphantly points out that there was no Congressional Flag Committee, or no record of one. The prosecution may be thinking of the present-day Congress, in which you need a committee just to send out for sandwiches, but in those days things were pretty primitive and sometimes Congress just did things. If Betsy lived anywhere near where she's said to have lived, it was a five-minute stroll from Independence Hall. If the weather was pleasant, Washington might have seen Ross on a street corner at lunchtime and said, "Hey, let's get Morris and go talk to your niece-in-law about this flag business."

The most ardent Betsyites claim she designed the thing for them on the spot, but that's nonsense. Francis Hopkinson designed it. He was on the Navy Board, and he wanted his ships to have some flags you could tell apart from the British flags, so we wouldn't be blazing away at our own navy. Back in those quaint and curious days this was the main purpose of flags. Nobody thought of saluting them till later.

We'd been making do with something called the Grand Union flag, ever since the first shots were fired in the winter of 1775–76. It was sort of like the British Red Ensign, with those Union Jack crosses in the top quarter, and quite a lot like the flag of the British East Indian Company. This was visibly un-American, but you might consider it our first flag, and some historians think Betsy made this one, and not the Stars and Stripes at all. John Paul Jones had flown it on the *Alfred* in December of '75, and passed it on to Washington, who flew it in Cambridge in January '76.

If those pundits are right, and the earlier Grand Union was the flag she got paid for – fourteen pounds, twelve shillings, and two pence for "making ships' colors," according to the record – on May 29, 1777, small wonder she was worried about cash flow. Eighteen months is slow pay even by Revolutionary standards.

Anyway, Hopkinson wanted something a bit different, and doodled up a new design, and on June 14, 1777, Congress adopted a resolution: "Resolved, that the Flag of the United States be thirteen stripes alternate red and white; that the Union be thirteen stars white on a blue field, representing a new constellation." Hopkinson sent Congress some bills for designing it. First he wanted "a Quarter Cask of the Public Wine," but they ignored him. Then he asked for twenty-seven hundred dollars, and finally for seventy-two hundred dollars, but they never paid him a cent. They said he owed it to his country.

According to legend, Betsy inspected the design and said it would look better with five-pointed stars instead of six. She showed them how to fold the cloth to cut out a five-pointer (flag buffs call it a "mullet." Honest.), and . . . well, let Canby tell it. "She quickly displayed to their astonished vision the five-pointed star; which accordingly took its place in the national standard."

Here the prosecution sets up a chorus of sneers. Five-point stars, they say, were no big deal, and any seamstress worth her thimble could make them, and besides, the number of points wasn't important; for the next fifty years six-pointers and even eight were as common as five. This proves Betsy was a myth and a liar, and should have known better than to have a grandson as easily astonished as Canby.

Anyway, not realizing she was a myth, she went straight to work, and when she finished, "the first flag was run up to the peak of a ship lying at the wharf, approved by the committee, and the same day carried into the State House and laid before Congress."

The next day Colonel Ross told Betsy it was approved and adopted, and she was to buckle right down on "an unlimited order for as many as she could make." She was delighted with this business boom until she realized, after Ross left, that she hadn't any money for all that fabric. Canby wrings his hands in retrospect, building up the suspense.

Cast into despair, she yet consoles herself that "the Good

One" has never forsaken her, and sure enough, back comes Ross with a hundred-pound note to cover start-up expenses, and our pious but spunky young heroine's worries are over.

At least, they're over for ninety-four years, until her grandson hauls out the story that's made her a laughing-stock wherever historians gather together to guffaw.

Okay, you ask, why *didn't* anyone mention it earlier? What about the long silence after Betsy's heroic feat; her absence from contemporary books, plays, posters, newspapers, music-hall routines, product endorsements, handbills, guided tours, poetry, portraiture, and achievement awards?

Shameful as it seems, it may be that no one at the time gave much of a rap who made the first flag. We now, quite properly, feel about the flag the way the French feel about their wine and the British about their Queen Mother, but at the time we may have had other matters on our minds.

Certainly we had an amazing array of flags. Our glorious Revolutionary army never carried the Stars and Stripes into battle, but they didn't slink around flagless, either. Each gallant band of warriors brandished its own, emblazoned with rattlesnakes, pine trees, crescents, shields, linked rings, horses, maidens, phallic spears, wreaths, eagles, Minutemen, and enough mottoes and slogans to keep a T-shirt manufacturer in business for life. Luckily nobody had to cut and sew all this fancy artwork. It was painted on.

Even the stars and stripes kept mutating. Ben Franklin once described it as having red, white, and blue stripes. Sometimes the stars were arranged in five rows of three and two, sometimes in three rows of four and five. By 1795 there were two more stars, for Vermont and Kentucky, and two more stripes; the flag Francis Scott Key was watching for so anxiously had fifteen stripes. (It was forty-two feet long and thirty-two feet wide and hard to miss even by the twilight's last gleaming.) When Peter Wendover came to Congress he was outraged to find the Washington federal buildings flying a patchwork of flags with anything from nine to eighteen stripes, and he made it his business to get the thing standardized. In April 1818, President Monroe signed Wendover's bill keeping the stripes to thirteen, and we could finally settle down to having a reliable national symbol to salute, burn, fly over used-car lots, etc.

By 1870, when Canby made his speech, we wanted to believe in Betsy. Betsy's descendants and various entrepreneurs wanted us to believe in Betsy. A nephew published a booklet called "The History of the First United States Flag and the Patriotism of Betsy Ross, the Immortal Heroine That Originated the First Flag of the Union," and a lot of people didn't even laugh. An obscure artist named Charles H. Weisburger painted *Birth of Our National Flag,* using a woman from Lancaster, Pennsylvania, to represent our immortal heroine. Instantly, copies of it papered the country's walls.

A committee organized in 1898 bought a charming place for the American Flag House and Betsy Ross Memorial, though any passing spoilsport will tell you it wasn't really where she lived and sewed. The Philadelphia Monuments Commission refuses to recognize it, or even mention it in polite company. Some say her house was torn down in

1857, some that it was really blocks away, but anyway the one we've got looks just fine. Restored in 1937, it's full of docents in colonial gowns and memorabilia like a thimble somebody found under the floorboards and a sewing box rumored to have been the gift of Francis Scott Key's aunt. Glassed-in rooms feature mannequins sewing flags, upholstering chairs, and puttering over a bowlful of musket balls. The kitchen table is laid for a typical colonial dinner of mixed nuts in a dough tray. The nuts are moldy and two flies are trapped behind the glass, but it's the thought that counts.

The halls and stairs are quite wide enough for two ferrets to walk abreast, and visitors greet the huge, airy souvenir shop with sobs of relief.

But why, pray tell, shouldn't she have made the first flag in spite of all this hokum? Colonel Ross was on Washington's staff, and his nephew's widow was right around the corner and needed the work. Apparently she wasn't bad-looking; he may even have had eyes for her. Or maybe he was afraid he'd have to support her if she went broke. Was Betsy getting the job really odd enough to make her a beautiful legend?

According to Canby, Betsy married again, and her new husband, Joseph Ashburn, was a seafaring man who got captured by some marauding Britons and imprisoned in Plymouth, England. He was nursed there in his final illness by his cellmate, John Claypoole. You'll never believe this, but this was the very Claypoole who used to date Betsy back in Philadelphia, before she married Ross. Ashburn died, and in 1782 Claypoole was released and went back to

Philadelphia to break the sad news. "The circumstances were such," says Canby, "that the old intimacy between John and Elizabeth was revived." Their "mutual friendship for the deceased . . . ripened into affection," and Claypoole became husband number three.

Now, *that's* a beautiful legend.

Lafayette Slept Here

Sometimes it seems as if every second American is a certified Civil War buff, but aficionados of the Revolutionary War are hard to find. After its Boston beginnings, it was more like a seven-year muddle than a war, with long pauses between battles. Much of it was fought in state legislatures and the courts of Europe, arranging for help, scrounging for guns and blankets, food and tents. Much of the armies' time was spent in winter quarters, waiting for the snow to melt, for muddy roads to dry and rivers to subside in the spring. Waiting for help to sail over from France. Then, when summer came, soldiers drifted off home to work their farms.

Heroically speaking, the Marquis de Lafayette was a bright spot – and even he spent more time begging for boots than he spent in battle.

Lafayette was the rich young Frenchman who dashed over to help us fight. Unfortunately, a quick survey of twenty-something college graduates reveals that most never heard of him, and most remember that we won the

Revolution single-handed. No doubt a wave of patriotism has swept the schools, leaving behind the notion that the ragged, disgruntled, dwindling, and sometimes mutinous Continental volunteers whipped the mighty British army with sheer moral superiority.

Alas, we couldn't have done it without a little help from our friends, without French ships, without Benjamin Franklin in Paris negotiating and Lafayette here with his imported regular-army troops.

He was one of the few people involved in the conflict with a taste for actual fighting. To the French secretary of state he wrote, "Remember that I love the art of war passionately . . . that the idea of seeing England crushed, humiliated, makes me shiver with joy. . . ." His father had been killed by a British bullet at the Battle of Minden before he ever laid eyes on his two-year-old heir, and Lafayette idolized the heroic idea of him and pined for revenge.

He was the only son of an ancient family, born in the ancestral château in the isolated backwater of the Auvergne. Here his grandmother raised him and ran the province, and the whole visible world revolved around him.

His mother called him to Paris when he was eleven, and Paris was a shock: there he was only a gawky, tongue-tied provincial. He couldn't dance. He couldn't even ride very well. His manners were barbaric. He was tall and red-haired, with a pointy nose and receding forehead, and someone described him as looking like an undernourished bird. His only popular quality was money.

When he was twelve his mother and grandfather both died, leaving him quite marvelously rich. His great-grandfather engaged him, as soon as he was out of school, to Adrienne, daughter of the Duc d'Ayen of the powerful Noailles family. Her dowry – not that he needed it – was over a million and a half dollars. (She was pretty, too.) Still, love and money aren't everything. Lafayette yearned for fame. He wanted glory, military glory, to wipe out Parisian memories of the time he fell down on the floor while dancing the quadrille, and how Marie Antoinette had laughed. But Europe was quiet. The only available glory was in the American colonies.

He persuaded Silas Deane, the American envoy drumming up help in France, to take him on as a general officer. Before he could sail, however, news of the American defeat at the Battle of Long Island filtered back to France, and the government banned all French officers from joining the losing rebels.

Undaunted, the marquis bought a 220-ton ship, the *Victoire,* and after various muddles and false starts he sailed – pursued by orders from the duc and Louis XVI to desist and come home – on April 20, 1777.

The trip took seven weeks and he was seasick most of the time. His wife was expecting their second child. He had disobeyed the king of France and his even more daunting father-in-law, but glory lay straight ahead. He was nineteen years old. Back before the twentieth-century invention of adolescence, life could begin with a bang, especially when propelled by money.

Lafayette impressed the Americans – and himself – by serving without salary, proving that he had, as he wrote, "no selfish interest." Never mind that it would have been odd for a glory-struck teenager with an income of roughly four million dollars a year to fret over paychecks. Never mind that vanity and a lust for applause from the drawing rooms of Paris might be considered "selfish interest." (Jefferson, who had no use for applause, sneered at his "canine appetite for popularity.")

No matter. He came; he loved us; we loved him. Even the curmudgeon John Adams called him "a nobleman who has endeared his name and character to every honest American." And his money was no drawback – he poured three million badly needed dollars into our war.

He was given an appointment as a major general and taken to meet George Washington.

"The majesty of his face and his tallness," the marquis wrote, "made him known immediately." It was love at first sight. The fatherless Lafayette and the childless Washington were locked in a lifelong friendship; the marquis later named a son George Washington and a daughter Virginie. He wrote that he and the general lived "like two united brothers in the midst of a mutual intimacy and confidence." When news came of the Treaty of Alliance with France, he rushed up to the father of our country and kissed him on both cheeks, an impulse difficult for most of us to imagine.

Still, he longed for more fighting. Aside from some clever strategies and skirmishes and the wound he got at Brandywine, he wasn't making the splash he'd hoped for. He pestered his mentor relentlessly with martial schemes. He wanted to attack occupied New York; he wanted to roust the British from Philadelphia. He wanted to distract them by conquering the West Indies; by liberating Ireland; by invading India; by invading England. He almost invaded Canada, but bureaucratic confusion delayed the plan until the ice over which he was planning to cross had dissolved into spring. In a phlegmatic war, with both sides apparently cherishing the liveliest distaste for bloodshed, he danced with impatience. How could he be a hero if battles were never fought, if armies retreated as soon as they caught sight of each other?

Yorktown saved him.

Cornwallis had occupied Yorktown with a massive force, and Cornwallis was a formidable foe ("I am devilish afraid of him," wrote Lafayette). It was the summer of 1781, and the British planned to cut the country in half at Virginia. Two imposing French fleets were converging on the city by sea, while Lafayette kept it bottled up by land. For the first time he had a solid command under him, fifty-five hundred French and Continentals and six thousand rather unreliable militia. He was offered more, so that he could storm the city himself, but he gallantly insisted on waiting for Washington to arrive and share the glory.

Cornwallis kept strengthening the besieged city's defenses and waiting in vain for help from British ships. Instead, the French ships came, bringing Washington. Rejoicing, Lafayette led the trench-by-trench squeeze on the fortifications, storming them by night with bayonets. On October 19, Cornwallis came out. He tried to surrender to the militarily respectable French, who quite properly directed him to Washington instead. As the defeated troops filed out, they too tried to ignore the shabby Americans, until Lafayette told the band to play "Yankee Doodle" as noisily as possible, to remind everyone whose victory it was.

It was the turning point, the decisive battle of the war. And Lafayette was, at last, a genuine hero.

He urged an immediate attack on Wilmington or Charleston, but no one was interested; the fighting season was over for the year. Bored, he went back to France to use his considerable influence for more ships, men, and money, and to drink the heady wine of celebrity. He was toasted and feted. Louis XVI and Marie Antoinette were ardent fans; she'd completely forgotten that he fell down dancing the quadrille.

In America, after the Yorktown coup, the war stalled. In France, plans lumbered into place for an immense joint invasion by French and Spanish ships and twenty thousand men, with Lafayette as second in command. Then, early in 1783, with the fleet ready to sail, Franklin's preliminary peace treaty was signed.

Probably the marquis was disappointed. Glory is addictive stuff.

He had thrown himself into the American cause, heart, soul, and pocketbook. The French Revolution was a different matter. He had once written of fighting for "that liberty which I adore, for myself more than anyone," but a rich aristocrat, a friend of the king and queen, is bound to have mixed feelings about a revolution dedicated to beheading rich aristocrats and kings and queens. Which side was he on, anyway? Both sides wondered. Both sides considered him a traitor, and he spent five years in prison.

While he was there, his wife wrote to him, "You are neither royalist nor republican, you are *Fayettiste.*" Maybe so. But however self-centered his reasons, he'd come when we needed him.

If the French were glad to see us in Normandy, the marquis was just as welcome at Yorktown.

My Friend Will See You in the Morning, Sir

He was a tall, bony, wild-haired man, and he faced his opponent at eight paces instead of the usual ten. He knew the other's reputation as a deadly shot, probably the best in all of pistol-packing Tennessee. He himself wasn't nearly as good and his eyes, though fierce, were weak, but he was here deliberately, even eagerly. He was to rack up a lifetime total of fourteen duels, and in most duels a slight flesh wound would end the matter, but this man he had sworn to kill. Their seconds stood by.

He let Dickinson fire first. The bullet struck him in the chest, where it broke two ribs and settled in to stay, festering, for the next forty years. Slowly he lifted his left arm and placed it across his coat front, teeth clenched. "Great God! Have I missed him?" cried Dickinson. Dismayed, he stepped back a pace, and was ordered to return to stand on his mark.

Blood ran into our hero's shoes. He raised his pistol and took aim. The hammer stuck at half-cock. Coolly he drew it back, aimed again, and fired. Dickinson fell, the bullet having passed clear through him, and died shortly afterward.

"I should have hit him," our bleeding hero said, "if he had shot me through the brain."

A costume melodrama in glorious technicolor from the archives of MGM? A paperback swashbuckler at the airport newsstand? Well, no. The year was 1806 and the survivor was Andrew Jackson, later our widely beloved seventh president, just doing what any gentleman would do. The spat had begun when Dickinson took the "sacred name" of Jackson's wife, Rachel, into his "polluted mouth" and escalated in an argument over a horse-racing debt until death was the only answer.

Americans like to think of dueling as antique, elitist, and purely European. Not our kind of thing at all. Our historians and biographers ignore it as much as possible. Only one American duel can't be politely overlooked in our textbooks, and such schoolchildren as still learn history learn that Aaron Burr shot and killed Alexander Hamilton. They're shocked. Accustomed as they are to random murders, the formality of the occasion and the importance of the players alarms them. How could a thug like Burr have moved in polite society and held responsible positions? How was it possible that afterward he went, not to prison, but back to Washington to resume his presidency of the United States Senate?

Many confuse Burr with John Wilkes Booth: assassins both. Nobody tells the children that the Burr-Hamilton matter wasn't a uniquely gruesome crime but quite an ordinary event. Or that affairs of the kind were faithful to an ancient code of honorable behavior and, by the nineteenth century, so essential to American political and journalistic life that the Reverend Lyman Beecher, father of Henry Ward Beecher, had complained that "the whole land is defiled with blood" and "we are murderers, a nation of murderers."

Nobody mentions that Hamilton, not quite the textbook's martyred innocent, had been a principal in eleven previous affairs of honor, mostly aborted, including dust-ups with the abrasive John Adams and the trigger-tempered James Monroe, and his son Philip had been killed in a duel.

We'd like to forget that only in recent times has our umbrage mutated into lesser rituals like libel suits in which honor is restored by cash instead of blood and highway wars in which rival commuters run each other's cars off the road.

Scholars suppose that duels took root with the most primitive judicial systems, when disputes insoluble by witnesses were solved in a trial by combat. The lower classes bashed each other with cudgels and staves in their customary fashion and the gentry used gentrified weapons. On the hazy theory that God identifies the good guy and lends him a hand, the winner, whether he did his own fighting or hired a proxy, was more than just the winner. He was innocent of the charges brought; he was honest, and the defeated man a liar; he was the rightful owner of the disputed land, or ox, or fair maiden.

The ritual battle moved out of the courts and into the world. Gallant knights in heavy armor challenged their fellow knights according to an established code and made the welkin ring with their blows. Personal combat appealed to young aristocrats with too much time on their hands and spread in spite of periodic bannings. Landowners laid out and leased special dueling sites, complete with bleachers for onlookers. In France, the judicial trial by combat went out of favor in 1385 and Queen Elizabeth I later squashed it in England (although it was not formally outlawed until 1819), but the private duel of honor, sometimes graciously attended by the reigning monarch, was just hitting its stride.

Young men from all over Europe slipped off to Italy to learn the art of fencing at the flourishing schools there. It was in Italy that the first manual on dueling, *Flos duellatorum,* was published in 1410, and every medieval gentleman studied it closely. Traveling fencing masters spread out and founded their own schools. In Germany by 1480 the *Fechtschulen* enjoyed privileges conferred by the emperor himself and established a tradition beloved by the military and students in dueling clubs until well into the twentieth century – perhaps, it's hinted, even today.

In 1527, Charles V, overlord of the Holy Roman Empire, said Francis I of France had broken a treaty and was "a stranger to honor and integrity becoming a gentleman." Francis challenged him to fight it out. Charles accepted. Their duel, like so many, fizzled away in preliminary negotiations and was finally canceled, but news of the plans between the two most powerful men in Europe sparked fresh enthusiasm all over. Dueling was plainly the socially correct thing to do.

Battles of honor with various sharp instruments became a favorite pastime in England, Scotland, Spain, Italy, Austria, and Germany. In Ireland it was even more enthusiastically embraced, and in France it developed into an obsession. Henry IV, who enjoyed dueling himself, by proxy, was alarmed enough to outlaw it in 1599, but his subjects paid no attention whatever. Even though an apology or a few drops of blood often ended the matter, in the ten years between 1598 and 1608, some eight thousand Frenchmen died on the field of honor. In the 180 years of its peak popularity, forty thousand of them bit the dust. Even the women joined in. In 1721, a Lady de Nesle met the Countess de Polignac with pistols in the gardens of Versailles over the handsome Duc de Richelieu. Their first shots went wild, but in the second round de Nesle was badly wounded. In the reign of Louis XIV, Madame de St. Belmont challenged a cavalry officer who had moved uninvited into her absent husband's chateau. Dressed as a man, she met him on the designated field and promptly disarmed him with her sword.

By then, the textbooks were less concerned with the fine points of swordplay than with the fine points of a gentleman's honor, of exactly when a challenge was required, how to deliver it, how to accept it, and how to emerge, dead or alive, washed clean of the disrespectful look, word, or gesture. The Code Duello was adapted in Ireland in 1777 and spread rapidly. Its twenty-six rules laid out the proper conditions for upper-class combat, the wording of challenges, and the right of the challengee to choose the time, place, and weapons. The rules were paramount; if they were broken, it wasn't a duel at all, merely an unseemly brawl.

Only another gentleman could meet a gentleman. Nobody could stoop to duel with the lower classes, who went on settling scores among themselves without formality, punching each other out as they'd always done. If a churl insulted a gentleman, the gentleman might have him flogged, but there was no way he could honorably avenge himself face to face. Not that it mattered much: a peasant's insult was no insult at all. Among the elite, however, no slight could decently go unchallenged and no challenge decently go unmet.

Like bungee-jumping, rock-climbing, and other dangerous customs, duels were popular because they were exciting. They offered the restless young an outlet for natural aggressions; they spiked the testosterone; they provided the heady rush of risk without the inconvenience of going to war. They impressed fair ladies. They impressed one's peers. They impressed those who might grant advancement at court or in the military; illegal or not, they looked good on the résumé.

Alexandre Dumas, writing in the mid-nineteenth century of the glory days of the seventeenth, gave the world the merrily fearless Three Musketeers, parents of dozens of rousing movies. (One of the three at least was based on a real firebrand, Armand de Sillegue, Lord of Athos, who died by the sword in 1643.) The young hero, d'Artagnan, is a Gascon hothead like Rostand's Cyrano de Bergerac, the poet who composed and recited elaborate verse while skewering his opponent. As d'Artagnan sets forth to seek his fortune, his father lectures him: "For yourself, your relatives, and your friends, never tolerate the slightest affront from anyone except the cardinal or the king. . . . Fight duels at the drop of a hat, especially since duels are forbidden: that means it takes twice as much courage to fight one."

Who could resist?

Duel-wise, America hit the ground running. The ink of his signature on the Declaration of Independence was barely dry before the brilliant Button Gwinnett was killed at twelve paces by General Lachlan McIntosh of the battling McIntosh clan.

Like so much of our Old World baggage, the duel underwent a sea change when it crossed the Atlantic. (One apparently English authority insisted, in the *Britannica,* that the duel on these shores was fought by drawing lots: the loser committed suicide. This admirably simple solution hasn't been otherwise recorded.) Here, fair maidens and a gentleman's honor were less of a problem than politics. The new country took its politics to heart, and all political factions considered all other political factions a threat to the republic and a personal insult. They called each other not just the traditional liar, coward, puppy, and poltroon, but fornicators, madmen, and bastards; they accused each other of incest, treason, and consorting with the devil. These debates often led straight to whatever secluded local spot had been set aside to soak up the blood of satisfaction.

To suffer an affront without challenging, or to decline a challenge, was political suicide, and these things had a way of getting around, by way of dinner parties, pseudonymous newspaper articles, or the purely American custom of "posting," popular clear into the 1890s, in tavern and streetcorner notices calling the coward a coward. Obeying the code of honor showcased a man's courage, integrity, and conviction and marked him as leadership material. It was a wise career move. James Jackson, at the tender age of twenty-three, killed the lieutenant governor of Georgia for his "overbearing" manners, and went on to become governor himself, as well as congressman and senator. Hamilton, explaining his acceptance of the Burr duel, wrote, "The ability to be in future useful, whether in resisting mischief or effecting good, in those crises of our public affairs, which seem likely to happen, would probably be inseparable from a conformity with public prejudice in this particular." A pompous way of saying nobody would vote for or listen to a cowardly poltroon.

Judges, governors, senators, congressmen, and rival candidates for office blazed or slashed away at each other. Up until 1800, Federalists dueled with Republicans. After Jefferson's election, Clintonian Republicans battled Burrite Republicans, and then went back to shooting Federalists. When Jackson became a bone of contention, anti-Jacksonian Colonel Robert Crittendon shot the Jacksonian General Conway through the heart on Bloody Island, near St. Louis. On the same spot the following year, Congressman Spencer Pettis, who was running for re-election, and Army Postmaster Major Thomas Biddle, who had called him a "bowl of skimmed milk," killed each other at the brutal distance of five feet. Among many encounters in the corridors of power, Congressman Jonathan Cilley of Maine and Congressman William Graves of Kentucky had a falling out over a newspaper article and chose rifles at eighty paces; Cilley died.

In the border states and expanding territories, pro- and anti-slavery hotheads challenged each other to combat. In California, the former chief justice of the Supreme Court of California, pro-slavery Judge David Terry, killed the anti-slavery Senator David Broderick before a large crowd of fascinated spectators. In the South, "abolitionist" was added to the list of words that required a challenge.

Policy differences rankled for years. Having disagreed about the War of 1812, and most other matters since, in 1826 Secretary of State Henry Clay and Senator John Randolph of Virginia finally met by appointment across the Potomac from Washington. Randolph showed up in a long flannel dressing-gown. (Considered eccentric if not downright nuts, he had fought his first duel in college over the pronunciation of a word used by the debating society.) It was a distinguished encounter, though not quite historic, since the statesmen missed each other, narrowly. Then they shook hands and made up. A good duel could be cleansing.

Political honor hung by threads as slender as mail delivery. When General Sam Houston was a congressman from Tennessee, he mailed his constituents some packets of vegetable seeds to plant. They were never delivered, and Houston called Nashville Postmaster Curry a scoundrel. Curry sent General White with a challenge. Houston said he wouldn't fight such a lowlife as Curry, so White offered himself instead. They fired at each other from fifteen feet and Houston wounded White severely in the groin. Whether the seeds ever turned up is not recorded.

Even Abraham Lincoln, that tower of common sense, was no stranger to the field of honor.

He'd objected to certain tax-payment policies of the auditor of Illinois, James Shields, and wrote a dialect piece calling him a fool, a liar, and smelly to boot. He published it, signed "Rebecca," in the *Sangamo Journal.* Shields stormed into the newspaper office demanding Rebecca's identity. (People often stormed into newspaper offices in the nineteenth century, often heavily armed, and pressrooms kept a loaded gun handy.) The editor quickly exposed his source. Shields challenged Lincoln and Lincoln accepted, choosing cavalry sabers, perhaps because his famously long arms would easily outreach his opponent's.

Everyone showed up as planned, on a sandbar in the Mississippi near Alton. Honest Abe sat on a log idly swishing his saber around in the air while the seconds, whose duty it was to try to mend matters, conferred. Presently a statement was agreed on, in which Lincoln was said to have said he hadn't meant anything *personal* in the article, including, apparently, just how Shields smelled. Then everyone went home.

Newspapers and their editors were always in the thick of the dueling scene, fanning the flames. It was their main function. The notion of impartially reporting the political scene would have been laughable; a newspaper was a partisan organ, fiercely praising its faction and calling its opponents monsters, consummate traitors, and contemptible scoundrels. When the editors' invention flagged, contributors pitched in, signing their pieces with *noms de plume* like "Vindix" or "Manlius Publius." A politician who couldn't find a paper to wave his banner was forced to start a paper of his own.

Opposing editors could be said to live in a permanent state of duel, and put on their pistols when they dressed in the morning. Challenges rained down on their heads. Pressed for time, an editor in San Francisco posted a notice on his door, "Subscriptions received from 9 to 4, challenges from 11 to 12 only." In little Vicksburg alone, three newspaper editors died in duels in a single year. In hot-blooded New Orleans, Dr. Thomas Hunt, perceiving slurs on his family name, killed John Frost, editor of the *Crescent*. In Kentucky the pro-slavery Charles Wickliffe killed the editor of the Lexington *Gazette* over an anonymous dissenting article. He was tried and acquitted, but the succeeding editor, George Trotter, disagreed with the verdict in print. Wickliffe challenged him, and was killed at eight feet.

Virginia editors had a particularly short shelf life. The two brothers who edited the Richmond *Examiner* in the early nineteenth century both died in duels. Edgar Allan Poe challenged one of its later editors, but showed up, as one source has it, "in no condition to fight a duel" – i.e., too drunk to shoot. In the two years before the Civil War, O. Jennings Wise, editor of the Richmond *Enquirer*, fought eight duels. A lawyer named Mordecai Cook killed Melzer Gardner, popular editor of the Portsmouth *Chronicle*. Richard Beirne of the *Richmond State* and William Elam of the *Richmond Dispatch* traveled clear to West Virginia to fight it out. John Daniel of the *Examiner* disagreed with

Edward Johnston of the *Whig* over a statue of George Washington: was it or wasn't it Art? In the inevitable duel, they both missed.

As the duel went West it lost some of its classic formality, and sometimes instead of the courtly letter of challenge delivered by a dignified second, a glass of whiskey thrown in the face would suffice. It flourished, however, especially in California, where a dispute over whether or not to send aid to the snowbound Donner party led General James Denver, secretary of state of California, to kill Edward Gilbert, editor of the *Alta California*. (This was another good career move, and Denver went on to serve as congressman and territorial governor, and has a city in Colorado named in his honor.)

Many Westerners didn't own the cherished brace of embossed dueling pistols in a velvet-lined box, essential to an Eastern gentleman's haberdashery. They used what they had, homelier weapons of broader use, including the wicked Bowie knife that could slice off a man's nose like butter. In Denver vs. Gilbert, the weapons were rifles at murderously close range. Around the same time and place, Charles Lippincott, editor of the *Sierra Citizen,* killed a lawyer named Tevis in a duel with double-barreled shotguns loaded with ball at forty yards. The effect was quite gruesome.

Even back in tradition-bound Richmond, weapons sometimes ran amok. Thomas Ritchie, Jr., of the *Enquirer,* for no particular reason called John Pleasants of the *Whig* A COWARD, in capital letters, and Pleasants had to challenge. He showed up with a pistol in each hand, a revolver in his pocket, a Bowie knife in his vest, and a sword cane under his arm ("lightly armed," as some sources have it). Ritchie had two pistols and a cutlass in his belt, a revolver in his pocket, and a pistol in each hand. Pleasants died bloodily and was so greatly mourned that Ritchie was actually tried for murder. He was acquitted, of course.

There were few laws against dueling before mid-century, and where they were on the books they were hard to enforce, harder to prosecute, and hardest to explain to a jury. Dueling was considered, even by the federal lawmakers, as the mark of a manly and vigorous society and necessary to keep rude tongues in check. Congress did make it illegal in 1838 to offer or accept a challenge in the District of Columbia, but in the same year Governor John Wilson of South Carolina issued his sixteen-page pamphlet revising and updating the Code Duello for American use. It was a best-seller, reprinted regularly for the next twenty years.

By 1859, eighteen states had laws against dueling. These had no perceptible effect. The indignant principals, their seconds, their attending physicians, and sometimes crowds of onlookers continued to troop out of town or across a state border or simply into a grove of trees to settle their differences.

New Yorkers typically slipped across the river to Hoboken, New Jersey, or Weehawken, where Hamilton met Burr. The dueling doctors of New Orleans repaired, like all the bloods of that mettlesome town, to "the oaks" near Lake Pontchartrain to settle disputed points – surgical methods, purges, poultices, and the proper treatment of typhoid – with sword and pistol. Then other doctors would take sides on these medical matters and issue challenges until the oaks shivered with gunfire.

Islands and sandbars were popular for their ambiguous jurisdiction. Richmond duelists headed for Belle Isle in the James. Vidalia, in the Mississippi, was the favored spot to settle things in Natchez, convenient for the citizens to row over and watch. Bloody Island served St. Louis. Memphis crossed the river to Hopefield in Arkansas to fight, and the citizens lined up on the Tennessee side with spyglasses to watch. Mid-river, on a paddlewheel steamer, was another oasis, and James Bowie killed a gambler in a duel over a card game aboard the *Orleans*. From Little Rock, combatants repaired to the mouth of the White River in Mississippi. In manly Missouri, leaving town wasn't always necessary; "Wild Bill" Hickok, ex-Union spy, killed Dave Tutt, ex-Confederate spy, in a duel in the town square in Springfield.

Most famous of all was the more or less official national dueling ground in Bladensburg, Maryland, a convenient mile or so beyond the District of Columbia line. Here, on fifteen vine-choked acres, an estimated hundred duels were fought. A contemporary called it "the court of last resort, in which weighty points of etiquette, social and political problems and questions of veracity, propriety and right were expounded by the convincing power of gunpowder." It was here that General Armistead Mason died by a shotgun slug from his cousin, Colonel John McCarty. It was here that Commodore Decatur fell.

Stephen Decatur was a brave and dashing naval officer,

and the Navy had long treasured its dueling tradition; a copy of the Code Duello was in every midshipman's handbook and no niggling official rules hampered naval dueling until the Civil War. In 1808 Decatur sat on the court-martial board that suspended Captain James Barron, and Barron went abroad to brood. Decatur became the wildly popular hero of the War of 1812 and author of the caveat, "Our country, right or wrong." When Barron came back and asked to be reinstated, Decatur opposed him. Barron called him out and they met at Bladensburg, eight paces apart. Decatur, forty-one years old and by all accounts as sweet-natured as he was brave, died that night; Barron lived to be eighty-nine.

Around 1857 the deadly thicket was cleared, plowed, and planted to crops with a strangely flavored heritage. Dueling, however, fueled by the Civil War and its aftershocks, went on undeterred. Indeed, the Civil War itself and the Southern response to it sometimes seems more an affair of honor than a war, involving more personal pride than public advantage.

It did leave a legacy of men with such unassailable reputations for courage that they could afford to refuse to fight, and gradually some began to do so. Public opinion, the only effective court, was shifting. People had seen enough bloodshed. In 1893, Joseph Bryan, Confederate hero and editor of the influential Richmond *Times,* rejected a challenge over something he'd run in the paper, calling the custom "absurd and barbarous." He was widely applauded for his stand. Times had changed, and though even today in Virginia men may "ask each other outside," accompanied by friends to see fair play, it's not the same. The exquisitely accurate hand-tooled dueling pistols were headed for the attic. As the twentieth century approached, politics became less central to our emotional lives. Machismo could be more safely unleashed in making money, and legions of lawyers sprang up to defend, less colorfully but more profitably, our good names in libel suits.

Maybe our Founding Fathers would be proud of us. Maybe they'd feel we've made great strides in honorable behavior. On the other hand, maybe they'd feel we've degenerated into a nation of greedy poltroons without spirit or conviction, unworthy to meet a true gentleman at ten paces.

Here and there, though, the tradition did linger on. In 1959, in Hollywood, Barney Silva, co-owner of a chain of Los Angeles restaurants, experienced irreconcilable differences with jazz musician Jack Sorin over one Dorothy Simon. Resolving to do the thing right, the two men marked off ten paces in Silva's living room, wheeled, and fired. Both died.

KARL MARX
Beloved Husband and Father

KARL MARX DIED IN 1883. No other dead man had such an impact on the following century or cost it so much money.

Generations of Americans lived obsessed by fear and hatred of his brainchild, communism. Marx was our modern equivalent of the devil, an evil creeping unseen among us, lurking in comic books and folk songs, seeking to snatch and destroy. Like the devil, he was dangerously seductive to some benighted souls, who had to be rooted out and more or less burned at the stake. He seduced entire nations. The whole of American foreign policy was dedicated to one cause: to stop the spread of Marxism and then to eradicate it.

What manner of monster unleashed this genie?

By rights, the rallier of the international proletariat should have been a workingman's son who struggled up out of poverty, not a rich lawyer's offspring who struggled down into it, but Marx was always cross-grained. Except in theory, he knew absolutely nothing about the common laborer and never held a real job.

His father, Heinrich, had a comfortable legal practice in the Prussian city of Trier, as well as rent money coming in from lands and houses. To protect his position as state legal counselor, Heinrich converted from Judaism to the official Evangelical Church and had his son Karl baptized at age six – too young to see religion as the opiate of the people. Karl was to be a lawyer, like papa, and went to the University of Bonn, where he was punished for getting drunk and roistering around at night. (Drinking too much was to remain one of his few recreations.) That summer, when he was eighteen, he fell in love with Jenny, the sweet-natured daughter of government counselor Baron Ludwig von Westphalen, to the dismay of both families. They were secretly engaged and waited seven years to marry.

Karl transferred to the University of Berlin, where he wrote love poems to Jenny, took up with radicals, and wildly overspent his allowance. His father, like fathers before and since, was forgiving but baffled, and wrote, "Your soul is obviously animated and ruled by a demon not given to all men; is this demon a heavenly or a Faustian one?" This fatherly dilemma would vex the world for 150 years.

When Heinrich died, Karl promptly dropped all thoughts of a legal career and switched his major to philosophy. He got his doctorate in 1841, but his reputation as a loud-mouth radical and critic of the establishment closed off his hopes of a professorship. He fell to editing and writing for a liberal newspaper, *Die Rhenische Zeitung*, which lasted nearly six months before he resigned and the government closed it down.

In the meantime, Baron von Westphalen died and, with both fathers out of the way, Karl and Jenny married.

The Prussian Civil Service offered him a job, but he dodged it and took Jenny to Paris instead. Here he busied himself with inflammatory writing, including a critique of the German philosopher Hegel in which he said the proletariat was destined to redeem humanity. (He admired the French Revolution and the way the peasantry rose up and beheaded the aristocracy.)

The article appeared in the first and only issue of *Deutschfranzosische Jarbucher,* which also contained a piece by Friedrich Engels on "Outlines of Political Economy." The Prussian government felt that enough was enough, seized all the copies it could find, and issued warrants for the arrest of Marx and other contributors if they ever set foot on Prussian soil.

Marx was now officially exiled. He was also excited by the Engels piece and began reading up on political economy and visiting with Engels, beginning a lifelong collaboration and friendship.

Actually, Engels was Marx's only real friend, but then Engels agreed with him totally and supported him financially for years, working in his family's textile mill. Marx didn't care for people who disagreed with him, or for people in general. Disciples he didn't mind, but even his most ardent fans rebelled at the necessary reverence. His surviving letters are rude, petulant, demanding, malicious, and full of complaints about money.

He was lucky to have Engels and the loyal Jenny. Both unions were fruitful. He and Jenny were married in 1843;

little Jenny was born in '44, Laura in '45, Edgar in '46, Guido in '49, and Franziska in '51. (Unfortunately, three months after Franziska, Marx's son Frederick was born, but he was born to the live-in housekeeper, Helene, and bundled off to foster parents.) Eleanor was born in '55. A stillbirth in '57 concluded the matter when Jenny was 43.

The baron's daughter was a model of wifely patience. Apparently she never blamed her husband when she had to pawn her shawl in January; when she pawned her silver, sold the beds, watched bailiffs seize even the children's toys against unpaid rent; when the children went hungry and couldn't go to school because they had no shoes. Apparently she never complained when her husband's writing got them thrown out of Prussia, then France, then Belgium.

With help from Engels, Marx produced the *Communist Manifesto* early in 1848. It called for the working classes in each country to get hold of the means of production, politically if possible, violently if necessary. Deprived of ownership, the ex-owners would themselves become working class, all would be equal, and history – which is nothing but the story of class struggles – would stop. So would wars, because "In proportion as the antagonism between classes within a nation vanishes, the hostility of one nation to another will come to an end." (Well, I suppose it looked good on paper.) Marx winds up with a flourish: "The proletarians have nothing to lose but their chains. They have a world to win. Working men of all countries, unite!"

Being much shorter and easier to read than his *Das Kapital,* it was a shot heard round the world and became the basis for communist parties everywhere. And once again Jenny started packing.

After they finally settled in tolerant London, a Prussian police agent was sent to report on Marx's doings. He wrote, "He lives the life of a gypsy, of an intellectual Bohemian; washing, combing and changing his linen are things he does rarely, he likes to get drunk. . . . There is not one clean and solid piece of furniture to be found in the whole apartment: everything is broken, tattered and torn; there is a thick coat of dust everywhere; everywhere, too, the greatest disorder . . . When you enter Marx's room, smoke and tobacco fumes make your eyes water so badly, that you think for a moment you are groping about in a cave. . . . None of this embarrasses Marx or his wife."

In London, Marx worked in the British Museum (except when he'd pawned his clothes and had to stay home) gathering material for *Das Kapital*. The first volume came out in 1867, in a printing of one thousand copies. One reviewer wrote, "This book is far beyond the intellectual horizon of many people." It did gather momentum, though, and was translated into French and Russian. The Russians were particularly interested. (Those who could wade through it did so and explained it to those who couldn't.)

Marx's health had always been shaky; he suffered from boils and liver complaints and insomnia and nerves, and spent a lot of time taking the cure at spas. He died in London at sixty-four. Engels spoke at his graveside in Highgate Cemetery, saying, "The greatest living thinker [has] ceased to think." In all, eleven people attended.

He died almost friendless, this obsessed and thundering bully with the wild glitter in his eye. The German-American statesman and reformer Carl Schurz wrote, "I have never seen a man whose bearing was so provoking and intolerable."

On the other hand, if we rub the dust from his living room window and look in, we find his daughter Eleanor remembering him as "the merriest, gayest person who ever lived, the man bubbling over with fun, whose laughter irresistibly won one's heart, the most friendly, gentle and sympathetic of all companions . . ." She remembered him telling his children stories, reading them Shakespeare and *Don Quixote,* and riding them on his shoulders. She remembered his children harnessing him to their chairs and cracking their whips while he pulled them around the room at a canter.

For those of us trained to see him as the root of all evil, it's an unsettling picture to hold in mind.

THE MAN WHO MADE GERMANY

MOST OF US RECOGNIZE photographs of Bismarck the Iron Chancellor, creator of modern Germany, with his huge soup-strainer moustache and the predatory glare in his pouched and hooded eyes. Only his mother would recognize the Franz Krueger drawing of him at age eleven. He looks positively elfin, with a delicate mouth and a peculiarly intelligent gaze. He looks as if he had a secret. He looks, frankly, *sly*.

He was. He was the first to call politics "a study of the possible," and when he grew up he was very, very good at it. "Politics," he said, "is less a science than an art. One has to have a gift." He did.

Otto von Bismarck was born in Brandenburg on April 1, 1815. (For those who care, he was an Aries, like Hitler.) His father was a Junker, a member of the ruling Prussian landowner class, a dull-witted, easygoing country squire. His mother came from a family of learned professors, the gifted daughter of a distinguished government adviser, former playmate of the royal family. Young Otto sprang equally from both sides of this misalliance, which must have been uncomfortable.

He considered himself a Junker, and he inherited the coarseness that came with the territory. He once wrote to a friend, "The chief weapon with which evil assails me is not desire for external glory but a brutish sensuality." Sometimes he ate so much he threw up; he drank deeply; often he had his hand up somebody's skirt.

From his mother, much as he disliked her, he inherited his poetic touch with words, his royal connections, and his genius.

Obviously he was a genius. No one not a genius can even *read* the intricate history of his time and place, with its endless mini-wars, its tangle of mini-states with names like Hohenlohe-Schillingfurst, and its alliances that shifted underfoot like sand – let alone manipulate it the way he did.

When he was six his mother sent him away to school in Berlin and he never forgave her. He claimed he'd pined for the countryside, but it might be that even at six he hated being pushed around. He had to be in charge, always, and never forgave *anyone* who tried to push him around.

His genius wasn't immediately evident. At the University of Gottingen he worked off his energies chasing girls, drinking, running up debts, and fighting at least twenty-five duels. In his first administrative job with the Prussian service he fell in love with an English girl and, without mentioning it to his boss, traveled off with her family to Switzerland, where he stayed for several months. When his boss complained he quit, saying, "I will play music as I like it or none at all."

Obviously he was never going to shine in an entry-level position.

Conveniently remembering that he was, after all, a Junker, he went off to manage the family lands in farthest Pomerania and take orders from no one. He did make the place pay, but he was bored sick, in spite of romps like seducing the village maidens, galloping around at night firing pistols, and, once, turning a fox loose in a lady's parlor.

He fell in love again, this time with a pious girl who converted him to Christianity. At least, he said he was converted, but he didn't mean anything *submissive*. He meant he was taking God on as a working partner. His behavior improved some, though.

The pious girl died and Otto fell in love with a pious friend of hers, Johanna von Puttkamer. When her father objected to the match, Otto wrote him a letter so frank and honest that nobody could have resisted. He'd already learned the power of honesty and often used it as a tool – sometimes as a sledgehammer – to get what he wanted.

Johanna wasn't very interesting or very pretty, but she let him eat and drink as much as he could hold and never, never tried to push him around. He loved her dearly. He wrote to a friend, "I like piety in a woman, and abhor all feminine cleverness." They were so devoted a couple that when he had a torrid affair in Biarritz with a Russian diplomat's wife, he wrote Johanna regularly with all the sizzling details. She was his only friend.

He began his political career at thirty-two as a congressional delegate when Frederick William IV was still king, and made his mark with savage, reactionary speeches delivered in a rather squeaky voice.

Next he was sent to the federal Bundestag in Frankfurt to patch things up with Austria. He was an odd choice for the job and blew cigar smoke in the faces of the Austrian delegates. Perhaps he thought they wanted to push him around; Austria was rich and cultivated, the land of Mozart and Haydn, waltzes and pastries instead of sausages and beer, and Bismarck was probably afraid they felt superior. After Frederick William lost his marbles and then died, the new king, William I, made Bismarck prime minister, a job he expanded to the hilt. He was a great monarchist and insisted that everyone and everything had to submit to the king except, of course, Bismarck, who ordered his poor majesty around shamelessly and commented in public that the man was simply not very bright.

His goal was to separate Prussia from the uppity Austrians and gather up all the little German states and weld them together under Prussia. His main obstacle was the surge of liberalism that swept Europe at mid-century. (Prussia had thrown Karl Marx out on his ear, but that didn't stop him writing the *Communist Manifesto*.) Bismarck's political heart lay somewhere to the right of Genghis Khan's, and he thought letting common people vote would be pure anarchy. However, as a student of the possible, he sometimes did things that *looked* liberal, like letting them vote for representatives with no power at all who practically needed permission to go to the bathroom. When the liberals banded together for reform, he neatly pulled their teeth by handing out medical and unemployment insurance and old-age pensions.

His best weapon was the growing sense of nationalism, with Germans beginning to feel more German than, say, Schleswig-Holsteinian. Whenever the commoners or the little states got fractious, he cried, "The fatherland is in danger!" and pointed out an enemy, within or without, and everyone stopped whining and pulled together for the cause. When he called the Marxist Social Democrats "the social peril," conservatives swept into power and attempted (though apparently unsuccessfully) to curtail the party's activities; when people muttered against him, he declared another mini-war. This is a splendid maneuver and still works just as well today. Nothing brightens a president's box-office ratings like an enemy, however faint or far away.

In 1871 he arranged for William to become emperor of Germany. The new empire consisted of four kingdoms, five grand duchies, thirteen plain duchies or principalities, and three free cities. (Later there were some African colonies too, but Bismarck never took much interest in them; he only got them to please the French by annoying Great Britain.)

Oddly enough, the conglomeration lasted for almost fifty years.

Germany was now so powerful that it made all the neighbors nervous, and Bismarck was clearly the most important man in Europe. Prosper Mérimée, author of *Carmen* and other romantic works, observed, "Unfortunately there is only one great man in each century and Bismarck is the one in ours." He was French, and he didn't mean it fondly.

In 1870 Bismarck suggested that the prince von Hohenzollern-Sigmaringen was the very fellow to be king of Spain, though he certainly doesn't *sound* very Spanish. France overreacted and declared war on Germany. It was a long war for the times, lasting nearly six months and including the Siege of Paris, when Parisian restaurants served zoo animals. The Germans won, Napoleon III was overthrown, and Bismarck added Alsace and Lorraine to his empire.

Bismarck's diplomatic machinations grew ever more complicated and his lust for power swelled with his girth. Then in 1888 the old emperor died. His successor only lasted three months and was succeeded by William II, familiar to Americans as the Kaiser Wilhelm of World War I. He was a very different kettle of fish and not easily bullied.

They didn't get along. Bismarck wanted to set up a military dictatorship with himself as its head and William purely for decoration, but William had other plans. Since Bismarck never did bother with support from the masses, considering them basically cattle, William had no problem asking for his resignation.

In retirement he wrote a book, *Reflections and Reminiscences*. It was beautifully written and full of terrible lies about his own cleverness and the misdeeds of his countless enemies, especially William II. He had a talent for slander.

He died in 1898, yearning for the days of docile emperors, respectful peasants, and powerful Junkers who never got pushed around.

Gladstone, the British prime minister, said, "He made Germany great and Germans small." Perhaps this paved the way for a much more ruthless leader to come along and tell them they were the master race and deserved the world.

THE SINKING OF THE *CENTRAL AMERICA*

FOR 130 YEARS, THREE tons of gold lay a mile and a half down in the North Atlantic, waiting for someone to find it. Someone did. Here's how it was lost.

Until Wednesday, everyone on the side-wheeler *Central America* had been having a marvelous time, and why not? Luxurious accommodations, great weather, and Billy Birch, the popular singer and entertainer, as a fellow passenger. "The very sight of Billy," the San Francisco *Alta* once said, "is enough to make a cynic laugh." Being generous with his talents, Billy had been making his companions laugh – probably even the cynics.

Wednesday evening, however, off the Carolinas, things started to go downhill. The wind and waves kicked up, children cried, and various passengers excused themselves to go lean over the lee rail. "I was so frightened that night," recalled Virginia Birch, Billy's bride, "I lay down on a sofa with my clothes on, and passed a very uncomfortable time, the vessel careening fearfully." It was a rotten way to spend the night on a honeymoon. Virginia and Billy had just been married in San Francisco. The next day they had sailed for Panama on the *Sonora* on the first leg of the trip to New York, where Billy had an engagement with Bryant's Minstrels, unlike the rest of the passengers, most of whom were returning from the Gold Rush.

In 1857, if you wanted to get out to California in a hurry to pan for gold, you took ship to Panama, crossed the Isthmus by train, and boarded another ship on the other side. First-class passage – $300 – bought you a carpeted cabin with damask curtains around the berth (steerage was only $150, without curtains). If you'd already panned and wanted to get back, you made the same trip in reverse. Close to three million pounds of California gold, worth about $15 billion today, came East this way, and that was only the recorded shipments; billions more made the trip in coat pockets and steamer trunks and duffel bags. The *Central America* was loaded with nearly three tons of it, which is fancy ballast, plus the passengers' own caches.

The three-part journey took twenty-three to twenty-six days, a lot less time than walking across Kansas, Colorado, Utah, Nevada, and California. (When young Oliver Manlove, a passenger in steerage, had traveled overland from Wisconsin three years before, it took him five months.) It was also more comfortable than sailing round the Horn. At least, most of the time.

By Thursday, all 578 people on the *Central America* had to notice this was a full-blown hurricane they were rolling around in. "On Thursday," noted Virginia Birch, "we passed another fearful day, the vessel rocking and pitching violently, and at night the storm did not abate, but dark-

ness only added to our fears." She was too scared to be
sick. Others were too sick to be scared.

The evening card games were canceled, to the disap-
pointment of Judge Alonzo Monson. Once Judge Monson
had lost all his money and his house, too, in a memorable
card game, but it didn't slow him down any. Chances are
he circulated around the cabin riffling his cards and trying
to stir up interest, but there were no takers. The ship's
captain, William Herndon, was his whist partner, but
Herndon had other things on his mind.

Nobody slept very well, and they all felt a bit seedy in the
morning, but the *Central America* still had her head to the
wind, which is where it should have been in a storm. Robert Brown was so impressed with the way she was taking it
that he made a mental note to wait for her the next time he
made the trip. That was the last kind thought anyone had
about her. At nine that morning, Chief Engineer George
Ashby found the lee bilge awash in water.

"On Friday morning," Virginia Birch reported, "the vessel careened over on her starboard side and we heard the
beams crack; shortly afterwards we were told that the vessel had sprung a leak . . . the captain sent a man down into
the cabin, who intimated our danger by asking for all of the
buckets and blankets in the state rooms for stopping the
leak. The ladies never spoke a loud word and kept perfectly
calm and collected. I never saw a calmer set of women in
my life; one or two asked to be permitted to share in the
labor of bailing, but were told by the gentlemen to keep
quiet and all would yet be well."

Around ten the crew tried to set some sail, but the wind

snatched it away like a hat. Ashby tried to keep the steam pumps going but the hold was getting wetter and wetter. The men lined up to bail and tried gallantly to keep the bad news from the ladies, telling them they were just working the pumps and not bailing at all, without explaining why they were carrying buckets full of seawater.

There are always a few layabouts in every crowd. Joseph Bassford later complained that several gentlemen broke into the spirits and got soused. "I know two of the passengers of high social and political associations," he harrumphed, "who refused to work, but got alarmingly drunk. So much so that their more sober companions had to put them in their berths." Oliver Manlove was grieved to note that the pious minister who'd been preaching on the voyage had locked himself in his stateroom on Thursday with a bottle of whiskey and had never come out.

At three in the afternoon the ship's engines died. Without power she immediately gave up the struggle and wallowed in the troughs of the waves, listing alarmingly to starboard. The ladies scrambled up to port and hung on tight to anything that was lashed down in a futile effort to right her, except for Amanda Marvin, who kept sliding down to starboard to peek over. Amanda was never seasick for a minute, and she was an incurable cut-up, although she had rescued the terrified Fallon kids from their cabin before they drowned in it. (Later she said that while Captain Herndon was "particularly mild and respectful in the presence of ladies," he was "altogether too easy, and wanting in the stern energy and fearlessness so indispensable in an emergency like the present." Being full of energy and fear-

lessness herself, she was probably sure she could do better.)
At nightfall, Ashby swore he would personally throw
overboard any man who wouldn't work. Ansel Easton did
sneak away from the bucket brigade from time to time to
hold hands with his wife, Addie; like Billy and Virginia, the
Eastons were passing an unpleasant honeymoon. Ansel
was tired and hungry and thirsty, and Addie remembered
she had a cache of biscuits and wine in their stateroom. She
broke them out and passed them around, and they were
most welcome to the bailers, especially the wine, the "liberal bestowal" of which cheered them up no end. Few had
eaten, being nervous or sick or busy with buckets. Besides,
most of the food was underwater. Two girls, Miss Lock-
wood and Miss Pahud, did manage some lunch by dodging
the flying dishes and hanging onto anything that wasn't
sliding away. Being eight or nine years old, they thought it
was all the most tremendous sport.

Saturday morning the men were still bailing, but now
water came in faster than they could carry it out. Annie
McNeill thought she was listening to the Atlantic crashing
outside, then realized it was crashing in the cabin. "We
expected to die," she reported gloomily. "We were ready
for death." (Presumably so were the fellows who'd broken
into the liquor the day before; no hangover is improved by
a hurricane at sea.) Everyone – except probably Amanda
Marvin and the little girls – was resigned to a briny fate.
Then, as Virginia Birch reported, "On Saturday, about
twelve o'clock, when we had almost given up hope of pres-
ervation, a brig was seen some little distance from us, and
she rapidly bore down toward us."

The brig *Marine* was in bad shape herself. Disabled, she was short on food and long on saltwater, and didn't have room for passengers at the best of times. No one would have thought the worse of Captain Burt if he'd just wallowed on his way, but he didn't. He lay by about a mile to leeward, ready to lend a hand. Calm no longer, the passengers on the *Central America* screamed with joy and hugged and kissed and wept.

The *Marine* had no boats that could stand the weather. One of the *Central America*'s had blown away, but five were still left, although in the excitement of lowering them one was smashed. In the best seafaring tradition, Captain Herndon ordered women and children in first, and no one objected because they assumed everyone would go sooner or later – a strange assumption, since the passengers would have been stacked up like cordwood on the little brig, which would promptly sink, but it was a consoling thought at the time.

Human nature being what it is, as soon as rescue was at hand some passengers got to thinking about saving their gold. Life is more important than gold, but gold can run a close second. Jane Badger waded into her stateroom and got twenty thousand dollars in twenty-dollar gold pieces from her trunk and stuffed it into a carpetbag, along with a pretty shawl she was fond of. The bag was too heavy to lift, of course, so she left it.

Billy Birch put Virginia into a life preserver and they went to their stateroom to get her cloak. There they found her canary, singing its head off. "On the spur of the moment," noted Virginia, "I took the little thing from its prison and placed it in the bosom of my dress. My husband remonstrated with me, hurrying me to leave the vessel, and telling me not to waste time on so trifling an object." She paid no attention.

The crew tied a kind of noose around each lady to lower her into the lifeboat. She sat in it, clutching the rope as she dangled over the side and swung back and forth, waiting for the boat to lurch underneath so she could be dropped into it. (A fat lady landed on Jane Badger, who thought her neck must be broken.) Children were held over the side by their wrists and then dropped, with luck, into waiting arms. Everyone got thoroughly soaked, even those who didn't miss the boat.

Poor Lynthia Ellis had been seasick every inch of the trip, but then she was a martyr to delicate health at the best of times. She was traveling with four children and wanted her husband to come along in the boat to give her a hand, but Ashby wouldn't allow it. (*Ashby*, however, eventually got in, and so did Alonzo Monson, the gambling judge.)

Getting onto the *Marine* was a scramble, too. Jane Harris got wedged in the ropes by her life preserver and had to be cut loose. Mary Swan was dunked three times before they got a grip on her. Appraising the new transportation, Alonzo Monson found a foot or two of water slopping around on deck and figured it wasn't much of an improvement. The first thing Virginia Birch did was find a cage to put her canary in. "The little fellow bears no marks of his late hardship," she recalled, "save that his feathers are disarranged from the effects of the bath."

The crew rummaged around and found five cups; sharing them back and forth, everyone had some tea. All the spare clothes were passed out. Amanda Marvin sat in a cupboard in a pair of trousers, looking, according to Almira Kittredge, just like a man. Amanda herself said she was dressed like that because she wanted to be allowed to help bail; nobody would let her, and she stamped around muttering under her breath. Angeline Bowley wore a sailor's white drawers and a blanket. Jane Badger got the captain's undershirt and boots, and Addie Easton wore his second-best hat. The rigging was aflutter with wet dresses.

All the women were safe, or at least off the *Central America*, and all but one of the children. Ricardo Oliagne, a little Peruvian boy, had been under Almira Kittredge's wing; he wasn't allowed into a boat, and nobody saw him again. The *Marine* had managed to take on thirty-one women, twenty-eight children, twenty-two gentlemen passengers, and nineteen crew members, and it was quite a squeeze. The cabin was only eight feet square, with almost no place to sit but the floor, which was waist-deep in water. The smell was fierce, too. The *Marine* was loaded with barrels of molasses that had burst, and the pumps were sucking up their contents.

On the *Central America* there had been some scuffling among the men for the boats. Ashby, the chief engineer, was in one; he claimed Captain Herndon had told him to take charge of it, although afterward he came in for some criticism. Joseph Bassford said Ashby pulled a knife and threatened to stab anyone else who tried to get in. Bassford, who had a knife of his own, stuffed two thousand dollars in gold in his coat pocket and jumped in anyway, knife in hand. The gold fell out and sank, but at least Ashby didn't knife him.

After reaching the *Marine,* the boats never returned. Amanda Marvin said she was sure Ashby hadn't meant to desert his ship; he had begged the men on the *Marine* to help him row back, but none would.

Back on the *Central America,* the men kept bailing for a while out of habit. Oliver Manlove met an old schoolmate bucketing away beside him, but they didn't have time to chat. Presently they quit, since it wasn't much use, and took to building rafts out of whatever they could pry loose. Captain Herndon went to his cabin and put on his full uniform, including his gold-braided hat. He'd always said he'd go down with his ship, and he wanted to be dressed for the occasion.

It was evening. George Dawson went to help some men launch a raft they'd made from pieces of the forward deck and some rope, and saw Herndon on the hurricane deck. Just before eight o'clock, two hundred miles off Charleston, Herndon fired the rockets that meant they were going under. When Addie Easton on the *Marine* saw them, her world went dark; she and Ansel, like Billy and Virginia, had been married just three weeks.

Ansel was standing by Herndon. As the ship went down by the stern, he saw the captain remove his hat. Nobody ever saw him again. Apparently he didn't join in the struggle for floating woodwork. He never seemed like much of a struggler, being a weedy sort with thick glasses and the look of a mild, ineffectual headmaster at an English boarding school. He'd once written a book called *Explo-*

ration of the Valley of the Amazon that was a hit; Mark Twain loved it. At any rate, he went down like a hero, and a small Virginia suburb of Washington is named after him.

Alvin Ellis, too, perished in the deep. Lynthia Ellis later married a banker in Ohio. Her boys grew up and went homesteading in Montana, as far as they could possibly get from the ocean. Alvin Jr., who'd been only three on the *Central America,* was a telegraph operator for a while and sent the message about another disaster, Custer's Last Stand.

When the ship went under, those who couldn't swim clutched at those who could and drowned them. "A large number of the passengers had bags of gold dust," observed Thomas Badger, "and some doubtless perished in their efforts to save it." He himself had prudently left his wife's heavy carpetbag of gold pieces behind. The fortunate Mr. S. Caldwell of New York had strapped twenty pounds of gold to his waist and found a door to float around on; he brought his bundle safely home.

Oliver Manlove had buttoned a two-hundred-page manuscript of poems he'd written in California into his coat pocket, but somehow it ripped loose and was lost. That was the treasure he'd brought back from mining; he had made only a few hundred dollars but he wrote, "I had been fully paid for my time with what I had seen and what I had learned." That Saturday of the shipwreck was his birthday. He was twenty-six, part of a roving generation of curious young men with a continent to explore. This was his first sea voyage and his first shipwreck, and he was making mental notes for future poems.

Billy Birch got hold of a floating hatch window. His

fellow passengers were sloshing around him, fighting over flotsam to cling to. Sometimes one bumped into another and began a conversation, only to discover the fellow was dead, still propped up in his tin life preserver.

Billy did the only thing he could think of: he went into his act. According to a fellow swimmer, he "mimicked the sea monsters, told humorous stories, in his own peculiar way, and on that frail bark, stretched on his back, bleeding from wounds, at midnight, tossed to and fro upon the angry waves of mid-ocean, he not only showed himself a true philosopher, but inspired courage in others, nor did he cease his vivifying harangue until an overwhelming billow choked his utterance."

Good old Billy. He didn't bring his banjo, or the props for his famous parody of *Macbeth,* but there he was, half-strangled in seawater, banged about by debris and corpses, entertaining an audience too busy to clap. Nobody named a town after him, but his performance seems almost as gallant as going down with the ship.

Meanwhile, somewhere in the neighborhood was the Norwegian bark *Ellen.* "I was forced by the wind to sail a little out of my course," recalled her captain, Johnsen, "and on altering it a small bird flew across the ship once or twice, and then darted into my face. I however took no notice of this circumstance, and the same thing occurred again, which caused me to regard the circumstance as something extraordinary, and while thinking on it this way the mysterious bird for the third time appeared and went through the same very extraordinary maneuver. Upon this I was induced to re-alter my course into the original one, and in a short time I heard voices, and on trying to discover what they proceeded from, discovered that I was in the midst of people who had been shipwrecked."

It was about one in the morning. During the rest of the night the *Ellen* plucked fifty swimmers out of the waves. Billy got aboard around three. Captain Johnsen tacked back and forth looking for more survivors until noon on Sunday, when he decided he'd rescued them all and sailed for Norfolk.

He missed a few. He missed Dawson, Grant, and Tice.

George Dawson, the man who'd seen Herndon on the hurricane deck, was a tall, handsome, black bachelor who had been working in Oreville in California as a hotel porter. Alexander Grant was a fireman on the *Central America,* and was now on his fourth shipwreck, one of which – the *Crescent City* – he had shared with Dawson two years before; the world was a smaller place in those days. John Tice was the second assistant engineer. When the ship was about to go down, he had grabbed a ten-foot plank and jumped overboard.

Hanging onto some boards on Sunday morning, Dawson saw the same raft he'd been helping to launch. Eleven men, including Grant, were crowded onto it and it was riding several inches underwater, but they let him hang onto a rope and float along with them. Later a couple of passengers made room for him when they fell over exhausted and drowned.

There was nothing to eat or, worse, drink. By Tuesday, some passengers were becoming unhinged, and Dawson had to stop them from drinking seawater. On Tuesday night, two more men were washed away. Meanwhile, Tice on his plank had a stroke of luck and found one of the *Central America*'s lifeboats, unoccupied, and climbed in.

On Wednesday, several more men on the raft drowned. A dogfish jumped aboard and the survivors grabbed it, but it was tough as wood. They managed to hack off some scraps to chew on, more as consolation than nourishment. That night, Baddington and Gilbert swam toward what they insisted was home. Only Dawson and Grant were left.

By Thursday, the dogfish had softened up and they ate it. Later in the day they saw Tice in his lifeboat and abandoned the raft to join him. By Saturday they'd forgotten about food, but their thirst was ferocious. Waves broke over them. Sunday night Dawson lay down in the slosh and wished he were dead. Monday it rained a little and they caught some in a bailing can and their mouths, but not enough.

Having tossed around for nearly nine days and covered 450 miles of Gulf Stream, the three men were near the end of their rope when they were spotted by the British brig *Mary*. She set her topsails, hurried over, and hauled them aboard – the last scrawny, sunburned, exhausted survivors, although Tice had simply postponed his fate; in 1878 he went down with the *Emily B. Sonder*.

Virginia Birch, Addie Easton, and Jane Badger were reunited with their husbands. The other wives were widowed. The wreck of the *Central America* sent shock waves from New York to San Francisco. The loss of gold rocked the unsteady banks that had been counting on its arrival; across the country, one after another failed. Men spoke of a transcontinental railroad. Others questioned standards of maritime safety. The confidence of a cocky era wasn't shattered, not yet, not until the Civil War, but it had suffered a hairline crack.

The *Titanic,* with its cast of celebrities singing "Nearer, My God, to Thee," later caught the popular imagination and inspired a whole industry of books, songs, plays, movies, and superstitions. Nobody sings of the *Central America.*

Till then, according to *Frank Leslie's Illustrated Newspaper,* "The *Central America* was the richest ship, passengers and cargo considered, that was ever engulfed in the waves of the sea." Some 153 lives were saved and 425 lost in 8,500 feet of cold, dark water. And, of course, there was all that gold, the bright harvest of the American dream, sunk too far down to glitter.

The *Titanic* passed into legend; the *Central America* passed into oblivion. Perhaps it's time to reconsider. Time to write her a song of her own.

America's Different Drummer

In the 1970s, Garry Trudeau's "Doonesbury" undergraduates named their commune Walden, and Zonker, the flakiest of the flaky band, spent much of his time submerged in the tiny but bottomless Walden Puddle.

Nobody asked to have it explained. Readers of the Sunday funnies knew exactly what it meant. They didn't need to dig out the book; the idea has stepped outside the book and shaped itself into the all-American daydream and a cornerstone of who we think we are. "Walden" means thumbing our nose at authority, respectability, and earning a living. It means simplifying life, and turning our backs on soulless human bustle, and marching to a different drummer. It means not just stopping to smell the flowers, but living in the flowerbed.

The dream surfaces and sinks during various cycles of our personal and national lives, but it's always swimming around somewhere in the collective unconscious. Probably it was down there long before Henry David Thoreau, but he wrote the book that gave it a name.

On Independence Day, 1845, an underemployed thirty-year-old New Englander walked a mile and a half down the road from his village and set up housekeeping in a shack he'd built by a pond. For the next twenty-six months he spent much of his time there – though not as much as he'd like us to believe.

He says, "I went to the woods because I wished to live deliberatively, to front only the essential facts of life, and see if I could not learn what it had to teach, and not, when I came to die, discover that I had not lived."

He also, though he doesn't mention it, went there to write a book, not *Walden* but *A Week on the Concord and Merrimack Rivers,* from the journals he'd kept on a rowboat trip with his brother, John. John had died of lockjaw in 1841, and Thoreau apparently planned it as a sort of memorial, but he didn't settle down to the job until he got to the pond, and as a memorial, it's missing its hero. Except for the plural pronoun "we," which may have been editorial, John might as well have stayed home. He never appears, not even in the distance gathering firewood, and never gets to open his mouth. In Thoreau's books, except for an occasional quaint rustic, nobody speaks but Thoreau.

Aside from some splendidly simple, lucid bits of pure description, *A Week* is an indigestible stew of philosophy, moralizing, history, and travelogue, interrupted by bursts of song. All through his writings, Thoreau refers to himself as a poet, and in *A Week* he tells us, "There is no doubt that the loftiest wisdom is either rhyme, or in some way musically measured. . . ." It's too bad he felt that way, because whenever he aimed his guns at poetry, he missed it by a mile.

Musing on American history, he writes:

> But since we sailed
> Some things have failed,
> And many a dream
> Gone down the stream.

In the bucolic mood:

> The western wind came lumbering in,
> Bearing a faint Pacific din,
> Our evening mail, swift at the call
> Of its Post-Master General;
> Laden with news from Californ',
> Whate'er transpired hath since morn . . .

Clearly the voice of a man who has mistaken the nature of his gift. Hard to believe the same pen wrote, in *Walden,* "If a man does not keep pace with his companions, perhaps it is because he hears a different drummer. Let him step to the music which he hears, however measured or far away." (Never mind that he was justifying what Emerson – and possibly his family – considered his laziness.) And of his bean field, he tells us he was "making the yellow soil express its summer thought in bean leaves and blossoms rather than in wormwood and piper and millet grass, making the earth say beans instead of grass . . ." Now, *that's* poetry. Maybe his reverence for rhyme made him nervous.

After *A Week* was turned down by several publishers, he paid $290 to have one thousand copies printed. Reviewing it, James Russell Lowell said that the rivers were made to "run Thoreau or Emerson or indeed anything but their own transparent element," and complained of being preached at. Four years later the author carried the 706 unsold copies home to store in the family attic.

Still, it had given him his reason to move to Walden and set him on the road to becoming a cultural icon and standard-bearer to the disaffected, sometimes called an American saint.

He needed Walden. He lived occasionally with the Ralph Waldo Emerson family but mostly with his parents and sisters in the family house; his mother was said to be domineering and talkative. He'd spent all but a few months of his life in this village where he was born and must have known every man, woman, and dog he passed on the street. In these alienated days this could sound cozy, but Thoreau was not a cozy man. As he puts it, "We meet at meals three times a day. . . . We meet at the post-office, and at the sociable, and about the fireplace every night; we live thick and are in each other's way." Simple claustrophobia gave him a good push toward the woods. He puts a nobler spin on it, though.

He wanted, he said, to "move away from public opinion, from government, from religion, from education, from society" and "meet myself face to face." He lived in what's been called the Flowering of New England, among folk who believed earnestly that the proper occupation of man was to become perfect by examining his inner self, glancing out at the world only to draw from nature the inspiring messages of a misty, nondenominational deity. Emerson, Thoreau's mentor and Transcendentalist guru, wrote, "The purpose of life seems to be to acquaint man with himself." Thoreau, in his journal, scorns philistines who "take cognizance of outward things merely."

Perhaps he had to keep reminding himself; the noble philosopher-poet was forever tripping over the lowly naturalist. Local legend held that Walden Pond was bottomless. Thoreau the poet should have left it that way, a metaphor for all sorts of profundities, but Thoreau the naturalist wrestles him to the ground and goes out and measures it. (It's 102 feet deep.) All those noble thoughts must have been a terrible strain on a man whose great gift and guilty passion was for watching, measuring, counting, and describing merely outward things.

And writing it all down. He wrote down everything, from the dates the fruit ripened each year and the thickness of the ice in the pond to the celestial nature of nature and the unworthiness of his fellow man ("It is very evident what mean and sneaky lives many of you live"), the debilitating effects of unchastity and what to eat for dinner. His journals over ten years fill six thousand pages in the printed edition, besides three thousand pages on aboriginal North America and hundreds more pages of nature notes. He rewrote everything over and over, even his journals. Even books already published. He rewrote *Walden* so often that his final version has vanished in the wallowing sea of paper. His writing was the talk of a compulsive talker who was never happy with social conversation – "We never ex-

change more than three words with a Friend in our lives on
that level to which our thoughts and feelings almost ha-
bitually rise." "How's your mother?" and "Hot enough for
you?" were beneath his dignity, so he takes pen in hand,
giving us Thoreau in endless argument with Thoreau, ha-
ranguing, justifying, interrupting, and contradicting himself.

In *A Week* he interrupts a tirade against priests and doctors with a description of canal boats, which he interrupts
with twenty-odd pages on friends and friendship that leave
the reader and possibly the writer deeply confused. Maybe
John's death is the fish in these murky waters but it's hard
to tell: "One goes forth prepared to say 'Sweet Friends!'
and the salvation is 'Damn your eyes!' . . . To say that a
man is your Friend means commonly no more than this,
that he is not your enemy." (Leon Edel tells us he had a
"disagreeable and often bellicose nature," and who can
doubt it?) In his journals he seems to feel that hate is a
major part of love and friendship, and in a poem addressed
to "my dear friend" says "O, I hate thee with a hate / That
would fain annihilate."

All geniuses, he says, live alone. Edel says, "Hawthorne
loved men but felt estranged from them, Emerson loved
ideas more than men, and Thoreau loved himself. . . .
Thoreau made of his life a sylvan legend, that of a man
alone, in communion with nature."

And there you have him, the self-appointed curmudg-
eonly hermit of the pond, shunning all fellowship, solitary
for two years with only the seasons and his lofty thoughts

for company, and economically independent, having built his own house and grown his own food.

It's a pretty idea, anyway.

Any small boy camped in a tent in his family's backyard is more alone than our hero and almost as independent. Despising the ownership of land – he calls farmers "serfs of the soil" – when he needs a place to build his house he uses Emerson's woodlot. (This was gallant of Emerson, since only the year before Thoreau had accidentally burned down three hundred acres of Concord woods.) Despising the ownership of material things, he borrows an axe to cut down a sufficiency of Mr. Emerson's trees. Then he borrows the tools to build with, which he looks on as generosity, permitting his fellow men to have an interest in his enterprise. He hauls the boards for his shanty in a cart, presumably borrowed. With a borrowed shovel he digs his cellar and in May he gets some acquaintances to help him frame the house, more "for neighborliness than for any necessity." The stones for his chimney and the wood for his shingles were, of course, Emerson's. Much of his furniture was scavenged from attics, possibly his parents'.

He cultivates his borrowed land but doesn't manure it, "not being the owner, but merely a squatter," and plants his garden, including the seed corn somebody gave him. A leisurely novice gardener, he seems to have planted some things that didn't produce – he calls them failed experiments – and his corn and turnips went in too late to amount to anything. He claims to have lived on "rye and Indian meal without yeast, potatoes, rice, a very little salt pork, molasses and salt," cooked over the fire of Emerson's wood that also heated the house. He adds, a bit defensively, that he "dined out occasionally," though actually he seems to have been a regular at the table of the long-suffering Emersons, and probably his parents and sisters fed him too, dinners paid for by his father's pencil factory. And no doubt beds were available in stormy weather.

He carried his clothes into the village for someone else to wash and mend, and notes that, a year later, he hasn't yet paid the laundry bill.

And always he marvels at his self-sufficiency, and how easily a man may live whose needs are few. Some people might cringe at having so self-sufficient a neighbor, but at least his needs *were* few: he didn't want to borrow your lawn mower or use your bathtub.

As for solitude, it's hard to see where he found it. After even the briefest walk to commune with nature, he comes home to find various visitors have left him small mementoes. Even in winter, the Irish laborers cutting ice on the pond come in to warm themselves, villagers come to fish for pouts, and a salt-of-the-earth Canadian woodcutter stops by to talk his ears off. At least one dedicated fisherman treats his house as his own.

Come spring, the place is awash in visitors. He's so close to the highway he can smell the pipe-smoke of passersby, and "Many a traveler came out of his way to see me and the inside of my house." He had only three chairs and often twenty-five or thirty guests squeezed into the ten-by-fifteen-foot house, marveling at his stoic solitude, though in summer they all repaired to the pine woods out back. ("I had more visitors while I lived in the woods than at any other period of my life.") He mentions girls and boys and young women, men of business, farmers, ministers, doctors, lawyers, housekeepers, young men and the old and infirm and timid, self-styled reformers, children come a-berrying, railroad men, fishermen, hunters, poets, and philosophers. Someone suggested he keep a guest book, like a hotel. Apparently he was a local landmark, a one-man resident circus, and the whole village dropped in to watch.

This was when he was at Walden at all. He'd like us to believe that from his house there was "no path to the civilized world," and yet somehow "Every day or two I strolled to the village to hear some of the gossip which is incessantly going on there, circulating either from mouth to mouth, or from newspaper to newspaper, and which, taken in homeopathic doses, was really as refreshing in its way as the rustle of leaves and the peeping of frogs." He walks around the village, inspecting the citizens and sneering at them for inspecting each other, and visits in various houses, often until late at night. He writes, "Sometimes, after staying in a village parlor till the family had all retired, I have returned to the woods. . . ." There sits our happy hermit all evening, so desperate for society that he ignores the yawns of his hosts until finally, overcome with sleep, they stagger off to bed and leave their guest in possession of the living room.

"I find it wholesome to be alone the greater part of the time," he tells us. He doesn't say how he would know.

In his second year by the pond he began to write *Walden*, working from his journals. His idyll was very briefly interrupted by a night in jail that inspired the lecture published after his death as "Civil Disobedience." This essay was definitely a shot heard round the world and influenced such unlikely bedfellows as Tolstoy and Gandhi, who named his resistance movement after it.

Thoreau hadn't paid his poll tax, as a protest against a government that tolerated slavery and engaged in an immoral war with Mexico. (In point of fact, the Mexican War had just begun and he hadn't paid the tax for six years, but he liked to get maximum mileage from a gesture.) He was locked up in what sounds like an unusually jolly jail and found the night "novel and interesting enough. The prisoners in their shirt-sleeves were enjoying a chat and the evening air in the doorway, when I entered. But the jailer said, 'Come, boys, it is time to lock up,' and so they dispersed. . . ."

A relative, probably his sensible Aunt Maria, paid the back taxes and the jailer threw him out in the morning. For the rest of his life various benefactors quietly paid his tax to avoid further complications.

Thoreau's ideas, escaping from their pages, tend to snowball. Inspired by "Civil Disobedience," the draft-dodgers of the Vietnam years met stiffer consequences than a night in a friendly lockup. Inspired by *Walden*, earnest people who headed back to nature in the seventies planned not only to wash their own clothes but to card, spin, and weave them as well. Gandhi planned nothing less than the fall of the British empire.

Scores of scholars still peck through the giant bird-feeder of the journals seeking crumbs of significance. It may be that we take Thoreau's ideas more seriously than he took them himself. He was a great browser among ideas, trying them on for size, to see how he looked in their colors. Walden itself wasn't a way to live, only an experiment, and after two years he simply walked away from what was to become a national shrine. The village was as crowded as ever, but he didn't retreat to the pond even for weekends. Been there, done that, as we say. Or as he said, "I had several more lives to live, and could not spare any more time for that one."

Disliking authority as he did, he naturally hated the idea of slavery and delivered an impassioned plea for John Brown. His fans find this hard to reconcile with his non-violence and disengagement, since Brown was certainly guilty as charged of various murders and armed insurrection, but maybe Thoreau was excited by the thought of a fellow eccentric; Brown was as eccentric as they come. (He compared Brown to Christ, which was definitely a stretcher.) Later, though, as the Civil War rolled onstage, he advised a reader to ignore "Fort Sumter, 'Old Abe' and all that," regrets that he's even heard of them, and adds, "Blessed are they who never read a newspaper, for they shall see Nature and, through her, God." He's lost interest.

As a moral philosopher, he lacked staying power and sometimes even common sense, and the heirs to his ideas would do well to approach them warily. He bids us turn our backs on church and state and make no social, domestic, sentimental, or civic commitments; dispense no charity; read no newspapers; join nothing. Work as little as possible. Despise all trade and commerce. Each man hoe only as large a garden patch as will feed himself alone; each man save only himself.

A fine way to avoid flu germs but not quite what the doctor ordered to heal our social fabric.

In 1854, after seven major rewrites, *Walden* was published by Ticknor & Fields in an edition of two thousand. *Boston Atlas* said it lacked heart and "Knickerbocker" called it rural humbug, but most reviews were quite good, considering the strangeness of the undertaking, and our hero enjoyed a modest celebrity.

But two years later it was out of print, as was *A Week,* and these were the only two books published in his lifetime. Before he died in 1862, he arranged with his sister for the publication of *The Maine Woods* and *Cape Cod.* And of course there were all those thousands of pages of journals.

He was in demand as a surveyor with a reputation for accuracy, a happy choice of occupation that took him out into his beloved woods and fields, where he began to yield to the siren song of reality.

Reluctantly. In "Life Without Principle," he says, in self-reproach, "Knowledge does not come to us by details, but in flashes of light from heaven." "What sort of science is that," he asks, "which enriches the understanding but robs the imagination?" Noncelestial nature wasn't noble enough for him, but he couldn't keep his hands off it.

Others agreed with him. Odell Shepard, who edited *The Heart of Thoreau's Journals,* deplored "the gradual conquest of the thinker and poet in Thoreau by the observer. The 'views as wide as heaven' are being 'narrowed down to the microscope,' as he had feared. . . ."

In 1993 another book came out, his first in 125 years. Island Press published *Faith in a Seed – The Dispersion of Seeds and Other Late Natural History Writings* by Henry D. Thoreau. A very different Henry D. Thoreau. A relaxed and happy Thoreau, who has given over preaching and scolding and rhapsodizing and taken up counting pine cones. The mere observer has routed the noble poet, and readers who found him hard to like at Walden could almost love this older, gentler man who walked in the November woods nibbling an acorn, crouched down to watch the infant oaks nurtured by the pine forest, and spent days releasing the seeds from a milkweed pod and watching them sail away.

There had been patches of solid ground in *Walden* that felt friendly under the reader's foot and concealed a hidden poetry, like the epic battle between the red ants and the black ants, and the hawk that made the earth feel lonely. *Faith in a Seed* is all solid ground, and radiates the peace that comes from finding, however reluctantly, one's real job in life. Loren Eiseley, who called him "a fox at the wood's edge," says he invented ecology and outlived his century; he discovered the stately progressions of natural order and the kinship and interdependence of living things.

When he died Emerson wrote, "It seems an injury that he should leave in the midst of his broken task which none else can finish, a kind of indignity that he should depart out of nature before yet he has really been shown to his peers for what he is."

Counting seeds, weighing, and measuring. Reporting the brutal, silent struggle for supremacy among different varieties of pines. Of white birches, he tells us, "You could carry the seed for 1,000 acres in a box of three inches cubed."

Poetry is in the ear of the beholder, and maybe some get goosebumps from lines like "What'er transpired hath since morn," but others will find they can't stop thinking about the thousand-acre birch forest carried around in a three-inch box. It echoes in the mind. Maybe the poetry had been lurking in his obsessive measurements all along. Maybe his real poetry, like his ecology, was a hundred years ahead of its time and marching to a very different drummer indeed.

THE MAN BEHIND *LITTLE WOMEN*

IF THE TRANSCENDENTALIST PHILOSOPHER Bronson Alcott had taken the slightest interest in earning a living, we would never have had *Little Women*.

It wasn't written for fun. Somebody had to be the family father, and the lot fell early to his conscientious second daughter, Louisa May, known at home as Lu. In a poem he called her "Duty's faithful child" – as well he might – but poetry makes a thin supper for a large family. Like his friend Henry David Thoreau, Bronson had a splendid contempt for cash.

The March girls in *Little Women* – Meg, Jo, Beth, and Amy – consider themselves poor, and pine for prettier clothes; the Alcott girls (Anna, Lu, Elizabeth, May) were genuinely poor and wore other people's castoffs, endlessly patched and mended and then cut down for the next youngest. In the book, the saintly Mr. March is a Civil War chaplain and works as a minister when he comes home, though he seems to have no church and no ministerial duties and rarely leaves his study. No doubt the description of Mr. March's relaxed occupational habits came about because Louisa had never actually seen a man working. Her real-life father toiled only as a philosopher, hosting Socratic conversations, lecturing free to anyone who would listen, and opening various doomed, eccentric schools. Even his fellow Transcendentalists, except for kind-hearted Emerson, thought he was rather a joke.

Sometimes friends brought food for the Alcott girls; mostly they lived on boiled rice or graham meal. (Luckily for the budget, Bronson believed that eating meat was the primary cause of wars. His daughters were grown before they tasted it.) The Marches have a comfortable house and a live-in servant. The Alcotts moved from cramped and drafty place to place, sometimes squeezing in with charitable neighbors. They begged from friends, did their own housework, and hired themselves out to do other people's; the faithful Hannah, like rich Aunt March and the generous Lawrences next door, is imaginary.

Mr. March lost his fortune trying to help an unfortunate friend. Bronson blew whatever he had on Fruitlands.

Thomas Carlyle, the English historian, called him "a venerable Don Quixote, all bent on saving the world by a return to acorns and the Golden Age." Fruitlands, near Concord, Massachusetts, was planned as the seedbed of the Golden Age, a commune where a group of pure souls would live simply, think nobly, and share everything. Apparently this meant that the menfolk stood around admiring Nature and asking each other deep questions like "What is man?" while the ladies picturesquely hoed the cornfield. Lu later wrote a funny story about it called

"Transcendental Wild Oats," but it wasn't funny in 1842 when she was ten. She and her older sister Anna and her mother ("Marmee") seem to have done most of the work; Marmee was exhausted and bitter. Fruitlands beggared them.

After the enterprise collapsed, Bronson made the gallant and possibly sarcastic gesture of applying for work as a day laborer. Nothing came of this, so he turned his attention to teaching his daughters, a periodic fancy of his. He asked them questions like "What is man?" and lectured them on moral perfection, and even by mid-nineteenth-century standards they grew up marvelously ignorant. Fortunately Lu could borrow books from Emerson.

Marmee got work in Boston trying to find jobs for the poor. This was of dubious benefit, since she was an un-dammable fountain of charity, forever handing out the last of the food and firewood. All the Alcotts caught smallpox from some immigrants she was feeding. She and Beth nursed a family of ailing children who gave Beth the scarlet fever that eventually killed her.

Lu wrote that the Alcott home was always "a shelter for lost girls, abused wives, friendless children, and weak or wicked men." Ardent Abolitionists, they housed an occasional runaway slave, and at various times most of John Brown's surviving family moved in with them. There was precious little privacy, and in winter it was grim indeed; Bronson considered an open fireplace more philosophical than woodstoves or furnaces. Whenever she could afford it and escape from duties at home, Lu's idea of a luxurious winter getaway was a furnished room in Boston.

By the time she was fifteen she realized that if the Alcotts weren't going to freeze and starve to death, she would have to start earning serious money.

Four occupations accepted women: sewing, teaching small children, nursing, and housework. Lu worked at them all, often simultaneously. The once-whistling tomboy sewed miles of seams, sometimes working till dawn to fill an order. She opened a school in the parlor, taught all day and sewed at night. She hired herself out as a housekeeper at two dollars a week, then a governess, a nurse, a laundress. And always she planned her stories in her mind and wrote them down when she had time.

She grew up among the Concord writers – Emerson, Hawthorne, Thoreau – and writing seemed a natural way to earn money. ("I think I shall write books, and get rich and famous," says Jo). Lu's first printed story, written when she was sixteen, brought her five dollars. "Great rubbish!" she called it. Not that she minded. Her ambitions were mercenary, not literary; her true love was the theater.

The early stories were the melodramas popular in newspapers at the time and fetched five or ten dollars apiece, duly recorded in her journal. Her journal entries are bare and businesslike, without the musing and flourishes we expect of writers, and every book or story mentioned has its dollar sign; she might have been selling potatoes. The only exception was a piece on Emerson ("the god of my idolatry"). That one she called a labor of love.

Sometimes Bronson did bestir himself. In 1853 he went "to the West to try his luck – so poor, so hopeful, so serene," as Lu wrote. Mysteriously his relatives, who should have known better, expected him to come home rolling in money from some unspecified enterprise. He did come home, in a snowstorm, half frozen. He had a dollar in his wallet and someone had stolen his overcoat. The family was, as always, glad to see him. Nobody held his uselessness against him, considering it a kind of incurable handicap, though Lu took an occasional dig and once wrote him that she meant to prove "that though an *Alcott* I *can* support myself."

In 1855, when she was twenty-two, she sold a book of stories she'd written at sixteen to amuse Emerson's daughter. It was called *Flower Fables* and brought in thirty-two dollars. Financed by sewing and teaching, her career wobbled forward. On paper donated by a cousin, she slogged away at collections of stories with titles like *Beach Bubbles* and *Christmas Elves* that would have gagged a less motivated author.

By the onset of the Civil War she was pining for change and excitement and joined the nursing corps. She'd wanted battlefields, but what she got was a crowded, stinking hospital in Washington, and six weeks later Bronson brought her home terribly sick and delirious with typhoid fever. She wrote later, "I was never ill before this time, and never well afterwards." However, the letters she'd written home were published in a newspaper and then in a book called *Hospital Sketches*. They were no great shakes as literature, but the public was hungry for war tales and she became quite a celebrity. Her prices went up. She paid off the family debts and treated May, the youngest, to drawing lessons.

Traveling as a nurse to a fractious invalid, she finally got her longed-for trip to Europe, where she met the Polish boy who served as her model for Laurie. When she came home, she found the family in debt again and Marmee collapsing under illness and work, so when a publisher asked her to write a "girls' book" she picked up her pen, though not happily: "I don't enjoy this sort of thing. Never liked girls . . ."

While nursing her mother and keeping house, she churned out a chapter a day and finished the first section of *Little Women* between May and July. Aside from the cosmetic surgery on papa and the added personnel, most of it was the remembered youth of herself and her sisters, the only girls she knew.

In real life Anna, like Meg March, married a virtuous if unexciting man named John. He survived the event by just ten years, leaving his two small sons for Lu to provide for, her third generation of dependents.

Elizabeth Alcott had died in 1858, less peacefully than Beth March. She was twenty-three and looked forty, and spent her last days calling desperately for ether, though by then it had lost its effect. The complications of scarlet fever were various, but it's easy to believe that with warmer clothes and a warmer house, a heartier diet and fewer toilsome hours in the cellar kitchen, she might have survived, to deprive generations of a good, hard cry.

It took Lu eight years to pay off her doctor's bills.

May – an anagram for "Amy" – was more talented and likable in life than in print. She was a cheerful person less burdened by nobility than the others, but no butterfly; she taught drawing, and Lu includes her with herself as one of the "workers." In her thirties, while studying art abroad courtesy of Lu, she met and married a Swiss and spent a couple of happy years with him, then died after giving birth to a daughter, Lulu. Lu, of course, raised her namesake. There was no Professor Bhaer to take care of the real Jo and release her from the "selfish, lonely, and cold" life of writing. Nobody, as she often mentions in her journals, ever did take care of the real Jo.

Little Women, part one, sold handsomely, and Lu tackled part two, determined to get it over with in a month. ("I won't marry Jo to Laurie to please anyone," she insisted. She had always resented May as the lucky one who got whatever she wanted; naturally Amy gets Laurie.) She finished it as 1869 began, complaining that "my headaches, cough, and weariness keep me from working as I once did, fourteen hours a day." Again the family's debts were paid.

Then she wrote *An Old-Fashioned Girl* and *Little Men*. *Shawl Straps*. *Jo's Boys*. *Work*. *Silver Pitchers* – "Poor stuff; but the mill must keep on grinding even chaff." *Aunt Jo's Scrap-Bag* (six volumes). *Jack and Jill*. *Eight Cousins*. *Rose in Bloom*. *Under the Lilacs*. *LuLu's Library* (three volumes). And countless best-forgotten short pieces at ever-escalating prices.

If Bronson was pathologically irresponsible, his daughter was pathologically responsible. Her first goal had been independence and basic necessities for her family. As more money came in, the goalposts stretched to include comforts – carpets and a furnace for the freezing house – and then luxuries – pretty clothes and Europe for May. A wardrobe for Bronson, who cashed in on her success and traveled around as "the grandfather of *Little Women*." ("Riding in Louisa's chariot," he called it.) Then the niece and nephews. A house for Anna. Total strangers clamoring for charity.

Marmee's last long illness wore Lu out with nursing, but she soldiered painfully on, taking morphine in order to sleep, writing and writing, obsessed with earning money.

Ill and exhausted, she died in 1888. Bronson had died a few days before. She was fifty-five. He was eighty-eight, having had a good shot at outliving his entire family. Perhaps the unvexed life of philosophical serenity is healthiest after all.

She had always written at top speed, never pausing to rewrite, leaving lumps of clumsy prose. Maybe with a different father and a different life, she could have taken more pains and risen into the first ranks of American letters.

More likely she would never have published a word.

The Boy Called Gallant

IN THE 1930s, a Civil War veteran made his way to the little town of Upperville in the Virginia Blue Ridge and asked the citizens about the battle there. He had come, he said, to stand where the gallant Pelham's guns had stood. John Pelham, he remembered through the fog of seventy years, "was one of the best-loved men, I think, in all the South."

He still is. Between Warrenton and Culpeper, near Kelly's Ford where Pelham fell, a marble shaft reads "In Memory of Major John Pelham. Like Marshall Ney/One of the Bravest of the Brave." A local storekeeper and his wife saved for twenty years to put it up. "There was never anyone like him, you know," the storekeeper told a historian in the 1950s. "The bravest, the most chivalrous, the noblest, that was John Pelham. . . . I said to my wife, 'We've got to do something to keep alive the memory of that boy.' "

No need; the memory of Major John Pelham of Jacksonville, Alabama, has a life of its own. People stumble across his name in a book or see his portrait, looking so

young and sweetly stern, and they are transfixed. Some of
them join the John Pelham Historical Association, founded
in 1982. They contribute to the association's newsletter
and gather to retrace his battles. When pressed for a reason, they seem unsure themselves. "There was just something *about* him," they say.

His wasn't one of the resounding names of the Civil War.
School children aren't required to study his career. In a war
that bristled with generals, he was only a major, com-
mander of J. E. B. Stuart's horse artillery. But if you sat
down to invent the perfect Hollywood Civil War epic, your
Confederate hero would come out much like Pelham –
except that you'd probably move him from horse artillery
to cavalry. Having seen a cannon on the courthouse lawn,
you would have thought it a bulky, unglamorous encum-
brance, compared to a horse and sword. You'd be wrong.
Under Pelham's command, guns capered and pranced like
blooded stallions. He whisked those ton-and-a-half field
pieces through mud and over rocks and hills, wielding
them with the flourish and grace of sabers. No one had ever
used them so deftly before; in fact, they'd been almost
abandoned in the United States since the Mexican War, on
the grounds that they slowed down the cavalry.

Pelham slowed nobody down. At Chambersburg, Stuart's cavalry rode eighty miles in twenty-four hours and
Pelham's guns kept up, ready when they got there to hold
off pursuers. Once he chased a fleeing Federal gunboat down
the Pamunkey River, galloping along the bank, firing his
howitzer. Another time, with a single twelve-pounder, he
held down McClellan's entire Army of the Potomac. One
soldier remembered the battle of Williamsburg: "Pelham's

artillery came flying down the road, Pelham himself leading at full gallop, passing through our lines of battle right up to the front, where he planted his guns and opened fire on the enemy."

He could make a single gun speak like a dozen, flicking it from place to place under cover until the enemy, feeling hopelessly outnumbered, fled. He could see at a glance the single, perfect place to plant his battery. His eye for the field was so true that Stonewall Jackson gave him the unprecedented honor of "discretionary orders" to choose his own spots. His choice at Sharpsburg (Antietam to Northerners), some historians think, prevented defeat.

But brilliance in an archaic form of warfare is hardly reason for immortality. Something else about Pelham clings to the mind and refuses to let us go. That's why I am drawn to the twelfth annual convention of the John Pelham Historical Association. We met last night in Leesburg for dinner and speeches, and today we are boarding a bus to retrace a series of battles known as the Ten Days of November 1862, fought all along the eastern edge of the Blue Ridge.

Half of us are – unlike most Civil War followers – women, and we're a mixed bag of all ages, gathered from as far north as Manitoba and as far south as Florida, though none of the British or European members has made the trip this year. A grandnephew and great-grandnephew of Pelham's are among us. The rest are here for pure, nonpartisan love. "I like John Pelham," says a pretty young woman from Connecticut, "and it doesn't make any difference where I'm from."

These people have learned everything there is to learn about Pelham's short life and sixty battles. They know the range and weight of each gun and whether it was smoothbore or rifled; they can recite the dispatches. I alone am ignorant as a tree.

In the bright blue and gold autumn of Northern Virginia we file onto the bus, some of us wearing Civil War touches, some wearing Pelham buttons. Peggy Vogtsberger – founder, past president, and newsletter editor – wears a "Cannoneer" T-shirt and seems to be everywhere at once, brandishing a clipboard. "This is the eleventh convention I've organized, and its going to be the last," she says. "We've had some great ones, though. In 1990 we followed Stuart's Chambersburg raid. Wonderful country up there." She dashes off to chivvy the stragglers.

Bus-borne, we squeeze through villages and narrow lanes that look much as they did in 1862. No Disney has yet moved in to recreate them; no one in mouse ears sells us souvenirs. Our tour guide, a local lawyer, knows rather *more* than everything: "All the books will tell you they lost three hundred one men here, but I personally already know the names of three hundred fifty-three." Everyone nods. Fierce researchers, they believe nothing they find in mere books.

I try to take notes but can't keep up; I've barely scribbled "1st Rhode Island" before the poor devils get wiped out in Mountville. I slip into information overload and lose my grip on companies, regiments, entire brigades. The golden countryside swarms in a nameless confusion of ghostly gray and blue, while on every hilltop Pelham's guns bark like dogs and ghostly horses scream and fall.

We stop to picnic under the great gold maples of Welbourne. This comfortably sprawling eighteenth-century house near Middleburg is now a bed-and-breakfast and a Pelham shrine. But it was the home of John Peyton Dulaney and his family when, in November of 1862, Pelham spent the night before joining Stuart at Bloomfield. In the morning he scratched the date and the initial "J" with his diamond ring in the glass of a parlor windowpane. He was called to breakfast before he could add the "P," and after breakfast he stepped outside into the war again.

The "J" still flickers in the windowpane like the shadow of a spiderweb, and under it sits his photograph, this hero we've been trailing, the smooth-browed beardless cannoneer who was always called "gallant" and always called "boy." He was "the boy knight" and "the South's boy hero." In *John Brown's Body,* Stephen Vincent Benet wrote, "That quiet boy with the veteran mouth is Pelham." Stonewall Jackson reported, "It is really extraordinary to find such nerve and genius in a mere boy." One biographer subtitles him "Lee's Boy Artillerist."

He wasn't a boy. He turned twenty-four before Sharpsburg, and the war was full of younger men, many of them outranking him. But it was a war of the bearded, and Pelham's cheeks were fuzzed only with soft blond down, through which pink blushes glowed when he was praised or teased. He kept shaving the down, hoping to stimulate something manlier, but he died before he ever grew a whisker.

It may have been Belle Boyd, most spectacular of Confederate spies and wildly, if temporarily, in love with Pelham, who recommended the young West Pointer to the dashing General Jeb Stuart. Pelham was to serve most of his twenty-two months in the war under Stuart, who loved him dearly and all but adopted him.

It was Stuart who first called him "the gallant Pelham." The name spread until even Lee used it. Pelham's own battle reports were modest, giving all credit to his men, but Stuart made up for them. "Daring . . . brilliant . . . incomparable," he wrote. "Heroic example and devotion in danger . . . indomitable energy . . . skill and courage which I have never seen surpassed . . . the eye of a military genius."

Still, the promotions were slow in coming. The popular Stuart introduced him to all the right people, which was probably a mistake. Having met the slender, pink-cheeked prodigy in person, the authorities simply couldn't see him as a colonel. "No field grade is too high for his capacity," Stuart wrote indignantly while Pelham was still a captain. After Fredericksburg, he protested again: "Pelham won his colonelcy on the field last Saturday. . . . Do lay his case with the strongest recommendation before the President." And later, "There are generals as young, with less claim for that distinction," to which Lee himself added, "No one deserves promotion more than Major Pelham."

But he was still a major, still called a boy, when he died at Kelly's Ford on March 17, 1863. (In an apologetic gesture, Richmond declared him a lieutenant colonel on April 4.) Perhaps Pelham himself didn't mind. After all, to have a remarkable talent and practice it on so grand a stage, to such applause, is no small compensation.

Neither is love. And everyone loved John Pelham. If people who just stumble on him in books can't forget him, people who crossed his actual path spoke as if they'd brushed past an angel. Pretty Bessie Shackleford, in whose arms he died, remembered. "There wasn't a single line of hardness in his face. It was all tenderness and softness, as fresh and delicate as a boy's who liked people and found the world good." Every town in Virginia seems to have a tale of girls who put on mourning and made the hazardous trip to Richmond when his body lay at the capitol.

A West Point classmate said, "He was easily the most popular man of the Corps in my time. . . . There was something about him that drew you to him." One man who served under him said his smile was like a little girl's: "a gentle, trusting, loving smile." Another wrote of his photograph, "A perfect picture of Pelham cannot be had, because his most remarkable feature was his eyes. In social life they were gentle and merry, laughing eyes; but in the animation of battle, his eyes were restless, and flashed like diamonds."

In a desertion-racked army, Pelham's men stood fast, hypnotized by the blue-gray gaze: "He would look at you. . . ." one said. "The biggest and strongest just wilted when he called you to account." And another: "We would have followed him anywhere. As a matter of fact, I guess we did." So might men speak who have served under angelic orders.

Jeb Stuart wept when he died; his letter to Pelham's parents is incoherent with grief. It was a nasty skirmish at Kelly's Ford – one of several clashes that preceded the great

Southern stroke at Chancellorsville. Pelham, cannonless, was galloping into the fray with sword in hand when a shell splinter caught him in the back of the head. After slipping magically through the shell storms of sixty battles, always commanding his guns, this time he'd gone out without them. Perhaps those guns were tied up with his destiny; maybe leaving them behind offended the gods of war, or whoever sent him.

The granddaughter of the hospitable Dulaneys, later Mrs. Robert Neville, was only ten years old when Pelham spent the night at Welbourne, but she never forgot him. When she grew up she and her husband built "Pelham," an estate on a nearby hill where the major's five guns had once stopped a Federal advance. Our bus pauses respectfully in the lane to admire the estate, but visitors aren't invited. Mrs. Neville, I'm told, set hidden trap doors into the staircase. If Pelham happened to come back and needed hiding – and who could seem more likely to return? – this place stood ready.

In the Welbourne parlor, the Pelham Historical Association crowds respectfully around the scarred windowpane. We want to touch it. Cameras flash. Everyone speaks softly. From his photograph, Pelham considers us gravely, beardless as an angel would naturally be.

Peggy Vogtsberger and C. J. Cochrane, the member from Manitoba, have been staying at Welbourne. "We try to spend a few days here every year before the convention," says Cochrane, an intense-looking woman who seems to be standing guard over something invisible. Nathaniel Mori-

son, Welbourne's current owner, is a member, too, not surprisingly. I imagine all three of them sitting in this
dedicated parlor, in the evenings, cherishing the chance for
a few quiet hours alone with their boy.

In the cemetery in Jacksonville where he's buried, the
United Daughters of the Confederacy put up a monument
that reads, simply, "Thou more than soldier." I'm not quite
sure what they meant, but whatever it was, I have an uneasy feeling they might be right.

There was something not quite canny about that
boy. . . .

The Travels of Manifest Destiny

ALBERT BEVERIDGE, THE DISTINGUISHED senator from Indiana, put it nicely: "The American Republic is part of the movement of a race – the most masterful race in history – the race movements are not to be stayed by the hand of man. They are mighty answers to Divine commands. Their leaders are not only statesmen of peoples – they are prophets of God. "

God intended the American people – the native-born, white, male, protestant American people of Anglo-Saxon descent – to have all the real estate we wanted, regardless of prior ownership. Anyone who tried to stop us was flying in the face of divine will.

Beveridge was speaking in 1898, about our natural right to the Philippine Islands and the peoples thereof, but we'd been obeying those divine commands since 1607, when we hunkered down on the Paspaheghs' hunting grounds of the Powhatan River and said it was really Jamestown on the James. By the time the phrase "Manifest Destiny" was coined in 1845 the concept was already dear to our hearts.

From the beginning we had troubles with European countries ignoring God's plans for the continent, but at least you could argue with Europeans, or declare war on them. Unlike the Indians, they were thinly represented here by trading interests and ambassadors. The Indians *lived* here, as if they'd never heard of destiny.

It's true they fed us. The early white settlers and explorers had the most amazing trouble finding dinner. Surrounded by fish and game and wild-grown edibles, we sat around getting hungrier and hungrier until some Indians came by with groceries to trade for blue glass beads.

Aside from that, they were most unsatisfactory. Even converting such as hadn't scalped the missionaries was disappointing. Many of them took to Christianity like ducks to water – they already had an entertaining variety of religious rites and they figured the more, the merrier, which wasn't what the missionaries had in mind. And as to the protestant work ethic, they hadn't a clue.

In 1841, when William Seward was governor of New York, he wrote, "Indians have generally neglected, if they have not despised, agriculture, and white men have suffered inconvenience from the neglected lands, and the community was benefitted in consequence of their acquisition." (Put simply, if your neighbor won't mow his lawn, you get to move into his house.)

We rounded them up and sent them west, and then it turned out we needed the west for ourselves. We kept moving out there, and once we were there, troops had to come to protect us from the Indians or move them elsewhere, and then more of us went out.

As we got farther west, we found that Mexico thought it owned a lot of the landscape, like Texas. That was when the editor of the *Democratic Review* said that foreigners were interfering with "the fulfillment of our manifest destiny to overspread the continent alloted [sic] by Providence for the free development of our yearly multiplying millions."

Who could question Providence? Surely not President Polk, a real-estate president through and through. After he'd snagged Texas and finagled Oregon from Great Britain, he set his heart on Mexico's California, which at the time included New Mexico, Arizona, Nevada, Utah, and much of Colorado and Wyoming. Some of this space was junk, but the San Francisco Bay area was a plum.

It was sorely in need of development, though, and, as the *American Review* noted, "This will demand a life, an impulse of energy, a fiery ambition of which no spark can ever be struck from the soft sluggishness of the American Spaniard. . . ."

Polk sent some troops for a spot of quiet trespass over the Tex-Mex border, and after the ensuing skirmish he told Congress that Mexico had "invaded our territory and shed American blood upon the American soil." While this wasn't strictly true – it may have been our blood but it wasn't our soil – sometimes a little white lie helps Providence achieve its plans. We declared war.

A few malcontents like Thoreau and Abe Lincoln complained, but we won. Polk thought we'd won all of Mexico, clear down to Guatemala, but this was impractical. There were *lots* of Mexicans down there, and maybe they weren't heathen savages but they weren't Anglo-Saxon either. As the southerner John C. Calhoun delicately put it, "Ours . . . is the Government of a white race."

The following year it turned out God was pleased; gold appeared in California and much of our population dropped whatever it was doing and moved out there to reap our just rewards.

From sea to shining sea, we were monarchs of all we surveyed. Except for those Indians. In spite of the best efforts of firearms, relocations, smallpox, measles, influenza, starvation, and firewater, they hadn't disappeared, and it was getting harder to find suitable places to put them.

In the beginning, it was decent farmland we wanted, and Indians could just be sent away to dry and stony places. But there's more to land than crops. Who could know, when we gave the Sioux the Black Hills forever and ever, that the place was any use? Then General Custer went nosing around and found gold there. (At least, that's what history tells us. If I know Custer, he wasn't the fellow to shoulder a pick or get all muddy sifting through creek bottoms. More likely he ordered some enlisted men to find gold.)

Obviously God meant the gold for us. It would have been sacrilege to leave it to savages, so white men came pouring onto the Sioux lands with pickaxes. The Sioux objected, creating such a nuisance that in 1876 we had to send troops. In the scuffle General Custer got himself killed – "butchered" was the word in *The New York Times* headline – not to mention 226 lesser folk.

The whole country simply howled with outrage. Custer

was a Civil War hero and a blue-eyed blond, and killing him was nothing short of an atrocity and a personal insult to all Americans. Retribution was swift and thorough.

After that, things got quieter. We'd filled in the blanks on our allotted continent and claustrophobia loomed. What else did God have in His pockets? Well, Alaska and Hawaii, for starters.

We'd bought Alaska, a.k.a. Seward's Folly, in 1867 for $7,200,000. We wrote the check to Russia, though it wasn't Russia's to sell; she'd just stopped by for the sea otters. Some thirty thousand Eskimos, Aleuts, and assorted other nonwhites lived there at the time, and the Russians had considered them all prisoners, confining them to their villages except when they were sent out to catch sea otters. After using up the otters, Russia put the place on the market.

We took over, and hired the natives to catch their seals and can their salmon for us. Then in the 1890s gold turned up and the white population tripled. The natives lay low. They were a scattered, disorganized bunch and nothing in their experience with white men had encouraged argument.

In Hawaii, the natives had the advantage of a central government, at least in the beginning. Their downfall was that, like American Indians, they didn't grasp the concept behind real-estate sales. American businessmen had been busy there since long before the West was won, cutting down the sandalwood trees. When the trees were gone, they bought up the countryside dirt cheap, planted sugarcane and pineapples, and imported enough contract laborers to outnumber the natives.

By the time President McKinley annexed it, we already owned a good deal of it and, as Congress said, felt for it "the love of a father for his children."

Closer to home, we'd noticed that Cuba was still a Spanish colony, in direct violation of the Monroe Doctrine, which clearly states that Europeans have no business in our hemisphere. Conveniently, the battleship *Maine*, parked in Cuba, blew up due to undetermined causes and we declared war on Spain.

Admiral Dewey sailed for the Spanish-owned Philippines and sank the Spanish fleet. The war was over almost before it started, and we found ourselves with Puerto Rico and Guam and the Philippines and a fatherly interest in Cuba.

Senator Beveridge called the war "the most holy ever waged by one nation against another . . . a war which, under God, although we knew it not, swung open to the republic the portals of the commerce of the world." Soon the whole Pacific would be ours – "an American lake," people predicted.

Some thought this was stretching our mandate a bit, the Philippines being a long swim from the California coast, but McKinley prayed for guidance and was told to accept them as a personal gift from God. If God gives you some islands, you can't just mark them "return to sender."

Strangely enough, the Filipinos didn't want to be ours, although we loved them dearly – when William Howard Taft was their governor, he said they were our "little brown brothers." Over half a million of them got killed resisting the new owners. McKinley called this "benevolent assimilation."

The twentieth century arrived and Teddy Roosevelt, for obvious reasons, added our little brown brothers in Panama.

Then European matters distracted us. Hitler came and went, and when the dust settled, the notion of empires run by a divinely sponsored master race had lost its innocent bloom.

Our destiny shriveled. Aside from some leftover islands, we shrank back into our borders.

Some of us still miss the glory days, though. Ah, but we were giants in the land back then. We gaze at the stars. Perhaps, in a distant galaxy, God has a planet for us, a planet rich in gold and oil, thinly populated by little brown – or possibly green – brothers in want of civilizing. . . .

How the West Changed its Women

In her teens my grandmother wore sturdy boots for roaming the mountains and canyons of Colorado. It was free for the roaming, and being able to go wherever you please – always with proper respect for rattlesnakes – may breed a different kind of spirit, a sense that your life is your own and all things are possible. With her boyfriend she went fishing, hunting, and camping. She was acquainted with Arapahoes, prospectors, and horse thieves. She could gut a trout while brewing excellent coffee in a tin can over a campfire. By Eastern standards she was unladylike and quite without "accomplishments" – she did not paint on china or play parlor music or carry a sunshade or write sentimental verses.

Married, she came East, where she was to spend the rest of her life, but she never did get civilized. She was always independent-minded, impatient with feminine chitchat, and indifferent to public opinion. To the end, she played a wicked game of poker and told earthy jokes that made her granddaughters blush. Once, when the power went out, she cooked a three-course dinner in the fireplace, pleased with her reawakened skills, her white hair wreathed in smoke. She was still western.

There was something out west in the nineteenth century, in the restless skies or the mountain creeks, that changed people. Over time, it changed the eastern women who had made the overland journey. It changed the children they brought along, and those who were born there, like my grandmother, were a whole new breed.

> O do you remember sweet Betsy from Pike?
> She crossed the broad prairie with her lover Ike,
> With two yoke of oxen, an old yaller dog,
> A tall Shanghai rooster and one spotted hog. . . .

The menfolk took their families west to make a new life. They went for the free land, or to escape from problems back home, or to look for gold or better chances for themselves and their children. It was an enormous migration and became a metaphor for America, land of self-determination, boundless possibility, and an inexhaustible frontier. They took the long trail with their eyes on the horizon, but many of the women, like Lot's wife, looked back along the eastward trail of dust.

Abigail Malick left her eldest daughter, Mary Ann, and Mary Ann's children behind. "I never shal see eny of you eny More in this world," she wrote. "We are almost three thousand Miles apart." She never did see them again. Strange as it seems in these days of instant travel, many of those goodbyes were forever.

In the East women had lived among women, supported

by a web of female relatives and friends who made up their emotional world. Kind female faces were there through troubles and childbirths and family deaths. To pack up and go west with only a husband for company was desolating, especially since much of a woman's life could never be mentioned to a man. They went off, often in tears, because they deferred to their husbands and fathers in all life's decisions. In the new lands, this tradition was going to change.

Abigail was already in her forties, and this wasn't her first move. Back in 1836 she and her husband, George, had packed their children in a wagon and moved from Pennsylvania to Illinois. Twelve years later, after Mary Ann married and produced three children, with a fourth on the way, word of the rich farmland in the Pacific territories went whispering through the midwest.

For some families, moving on was to become a way of life. Our best-known pioneer family, in Laura Ingalls Wilder's *Little House* books, moved from New York State to the big woods of Wisconsin to Indian Territory to Minnesota, and then on to the Dakota prairie. Pa Ingalls, an otherwise responsible and conscientious man, disliked seeing a neighbor's chimney-smoke.

Abigail and George set out with nineteen-year-old Charles, seventeen-year-old Hiram, fourteen-year-old Rachel, and the young ones, Shindel, Jane, and Susan, aged ten, eight, and three. It was March 1848, and the trip in those early days took six months, racing to beat the autumn snows to the western mountain passes.

Halfway there Hiram, who had been looking forward so eagerly to the West, drowned in the Platte River. It was a year and a half before Abigail managed to write to Mary Ann, saying, "It has Almost kild me but I have to bear it." For mothers, the journey was an anxious one. Women drove the teams, packed and unpacked the wagons, helped lift them over rocks or hold them back on downgrades, carried water, dried wet bedclothes, gathered buffalo chips for fires, and squatted in the smoke trying to cook a meal, then washed the plates and scoured the pans. About one-fifth of them were pregnant, and many gave birth along the trail.

Not surprisingly, children were only roughly supervised and the older ones scampered off to get into trouble. They got trampled by oxen or crushed in buffalo stampedes, fell out of wagons or into rivers, got lost or left behind, and came down with mumps, measles, whooping cough, fevers, toothaches, snakebite, broken arms, cholera, typhoid, and smallpox. Everyone had dysentery – the "bloody flux" – and no privacy in which to have it. Shallow graves were scratched in the hard dirt and then the wagons moved on.

Lucy Henderson Deady wrote, "Three days after my little sister Lettie drank the laudanum and died we stopped for a few hours, and my sister Olivia was born." For Lucy's mother, getting there was far from half the fun.

The young remembered a different story. Susan Parrish wrote, "We were [a] happy care-free lot of young people. . . . It was a continuous picnic and excitement was plentiful." Miriam Thompson, eighteen and newly married, was "possessed with a spirit of adventure and a desire to see what was new and strange." Caroline Richardson, after a rousing snowball fight in the South Pass of the Rockies, "pitched a tent in a potato patch . . . Found a fiddler . . . and got together enough people for two sets of cotillions. . . . Danced till eleven." Ready to hit the ground running, they learned to ride, shoot, and trade with the Indians. It was these gallant, lighthearted girls who had time to notice the astonishing beauty of the unspoiled West, its mountains and rivers and acres of wildflowers. Especially the wildflowers. Even the mothers jumped down from the wagons to pick armfuls. Lillie Marcks, who was seven on the trail, remembered, ". . . to my mother and me it was a real lark. . . . Mother would say, 'Oh, how beautiful.' . . . The wild flowers covered the prairies in a riot of colors like a beautiful rug."

Abigail and George, early and lucky, staked the claim of a farmer's dreams. No droughts or blizzards would blight this rich land in the mild air of what would become Washington State, generous with salmon and timber. Resilient Abigail wrote her daughter, "We have got Abutiful claim near fort vancouver on the Columbia River. A whol sexsion of land, there is ships asailing every day on the greate Columbia right befoure our dore . . . we have an exceedingly Butiful Winter . . . It is a Great Country for wheat and the prettiest wheat that ever I seen . . . O it will be one of the gratest places in the whole world sur." She had fallen in love, and the loss of Mary Ann and Hiram was comforted by the new land.

The West was potent magic. Mrs. W. B. Caton wrote, "To say I wept bitterly would but faintly express the ocean of tears I shed on leaving my beloved home and state to take up residence in the 'wild and wooly West.' However, my fears vanished as we traveled toward our Mecca. . . . As we gazed with rapture over the beautiful valley, encircled by a fine stream of water, we felt that instead of the wild West, we had found God's own country, and were quite content to accept it as our future home."

The Malicks had come with all the necessary skills to work their claim and build their home, and prosperity came easily. "Our house is ful of good things," Abigail wrote. She sold milk, butter, eggs, and poultry. The pioneer women found that not only were their traditional home-making skills doubly valuable in the raw country, they could also earn money. Besides selling their farm and garden surplus, they ran general stores, trading posts, hotels, and boardinghouses, taught in the little schools, cooked and laundered for hordes of bachelors, and worked on newspapers or as postmistresses and seamstresses. The new cattle and mining towns made work for prostitutes, barmaids, and dance-hall girls. With money of their own, women took a firmer grip on their own destinies. Self-reliance became a pleasure as well as a necessity.

They were far from the feminine network that had been their emotional support, and often the physical support they expected from men failed, too. Young Jennie Marcy, left to cope with marauding Texas longhorns, lamented, "Why were the men always away when terrible things happened!" Cattle stampedes, prairie fires, Indian raids, floods, tornadoes, blizzards, childbirth, wolves, bears, drunken cowboys – they coped because they had to, and it made them strong. Men died or were killed or drifted off to the goldfields or into surveying or railroad work, and women worked their claims alone. Deference to male authority was fading fast.

Almost as soon as the Malicks arrived, a different and much shinier thread was woven into the fabric – gold. Gold fever shook the whole world, and the goldfields were close enough so that even hard-working George left the farm to Abigail and went prospecting with nineteen-year-old Charles. Perhaps unfortunately, they were lucky. They came home with gold, and George went back to his wheat and potatoes, but Charles, who had made five thousand dollars in a few months, went back for more.

Abigail wrote to Mary Ann: "There were peopple that knew Charles And said that Charles had Agreate deal of money. One said that he [had] seven thousand dollars. And . . . Charles was on his way home And . . . was Robed. And that was the Caus of his death." Years later, there was reason to doubt the "peopple." Charles may not have died after all, but simply vanished into the great western spaces as so many did, drunk with opportunities. And if he had come home, would he have stayed? How long would he have plowed with his father when faster fortunes were ready to be made? The dangerous new idea ran loose among a people already restless with westering. Every young man had reason to believe he could be a millionaire by morning. A lucky strike, or even a lucky poker hand, would bring in more than years of planting wheat. Gambling as well as gold-hunting became endemic, shaping the new generation. Mothers who had hoped to depend on sons to farm were left behind to depend on themselves.

For a girl, one of the great opportunities of the West was the wide choice of husbands in a land of bachelors. She needn't even stick with the first one; she could divorce and try again. Divorce became commonplace in the western states, and Susan Malick was a divorcee at sixteen. It was another option for shaping one's own life.

The three youngest Malicks were frontier children. Frontier children were a handful. Their mothers had changed and toughened their expectations of themselves, but they still expected to raise ladylike daughters and hard-working sons. Far from the world of traditional authority and obedience, these youngsters slipped through the parental fingers. For one thing, they were never home. Without porcelain dolls and tin soldiers to play with under watchful eyes, they simply ran outdoors and stayed there, making mud figurines, exploring the creeks, and taming a succession of pets from prairie dogs to buffalo calves. From the evidence of their memoirs, nothing short of a full-strength blizzard drove them indoors.

A new kind of little girl sprang up, suntanned, windblown, strong as a mustang, and independent as a mule. Laura Ingalls would always rather work outdoors with her father than stay in and help mother, and so would Caddie Woodlawn, in Carol Ryrie Brink's book about her grandmother's childhood in Wisconsin. Laura and Caddie both had educated mothers with strong ideas on ladylike behavior, but these daughters were something new. Caddie ran wild with her brothers, made Indian friends, climbed trees, caught snakes, went fishing, plowing, and harvesting cranberries from a canoe, and galloped around bareback.

"Our joy rides were horseback rides!" wrote Catherine Cavender. "Wild dashes across the prairie, the wind painting our cheeks with nature's red!" How could you supervise a daughter who jumped on her pony and streaked away into the wild country? Jane Malick went riding with Henry Pearson ("Oh he is such a splended rider") and was three months pregnant when they married.

In 1854, George had a stroke and died, leaving the "butiful claim" short-handed. Shindel, the youngest son, was a frontier child with a vengeance. Early on, Abigail had written, "He is a very rued boy and I Cannot do eney thing with him." At fourteen, he was hanging around Fort Vancouver learning a thing or two about gambling and horseracing. When he was seventeen he went off to the gold mines, leaving his mother to cope with the farm and an Indian uprising.

"Shindl is never At home to help Me enney. I have the Cattel And every thing to do Myself. O the hogs Are A holoing now for fead. I must go And feed them And it is Araning as hard As it can." From time to time he came home to sponge money from her. "He had spent All he had A gambling And had not got him self one bit of Cloathes And has loiterd Around ever since. . . . And wastes All that he Can get his handes on And will not even help to Milk the Cowes unless I drive him to it. . . . He will start up town And gamble All night. . . . I have oferd him Almost everything to go to school but he will not And he cannot hardley read one Bit."

When last heard from, he was somewhere in Idaho. The frontier had promised the parents a chance for a new life, but its children wanted unlimited new lives – lives to be turned in like poker hands and redealt over and over. Not just one opportunity, but a whole world of chances.

Susan, the youngest, eloped, left her husband when he threatened to cut her throat, and went off to be "An Actress in A theater trupe." Then she left the troupe, divorced the throat-cutter, and at sixteen was running a dry-goods store in Walla Walla. Five years later she had married again, her new husband had been killed, and her daughter was born. When last heard from she, too, was in Idaho, at the Boise Mines, far from home. "Home," for the frontier children, was not a compelling concept.

Abigail was alone in her last years. She still wrote to Mary Ann, still complained about her wild crop of frontier children, but more and more she wrote about her land. She had worked it, and managed to hold it alone, and in the end she loved it more than she loved her family. Her last letter said, "In About two or thre years More We Will Have An Abundance of chois Fruit. Pears And Apples And plums and Siberian Crab[apple]s And peaches and Cheryes of difrent kindes and Chois Apples Sutch As I Never Saw Eny In the states. . . . And four pare trees And I do not know how Meny peach trees And rasing More All the time." It must have looked rather like heaven in blossom time, this world she had created for herself.

She had had seven children. After she died in 1865, not one of them came to live on her farm, to drive her beautiful "teem of Creem colored horses" and eat her peaches and pears. She had found the independence the West had promised, but so had her children. They had scattered to shape and re-shape Western destinies of their own. That was what the West was about.

The Gravy Trains

WHEN, IN THE WANING YEARS of the last century, E. H. Harriman's doctor ordered him to take a vacation, the railroad king remembered he'd always wanted to kill a Kodiak bear and made some travel plans accordingly.

First he chartered a steamship and had it gutted and recreated as a luxury liner with a crew of sixty-five. Then he collected a team of scientists, including conservationist John Muir and naturalist John Burroughs, and various friends and relations, his doctor, three artists, two photographers, two stenographers, two taxidermists, a chaplain, and plenty of hunters and trappers. Then he piled the party of 126 onto his train, the Utopia, at Grand Central Station in New York City and set out toward the Seattle-docked ship.

The royal progress crossed the country, pausing from time to time to see the Shoshone Falls or the Snake River or take the saddle horses out of the cattle cars and go for a gallop. From Seattle their ship, stocked with mountains of scientific gear, milk cows, pigs, live chickens, grapefruit, and oranges, sailed for Alaska, where the party explored for two months.

They saw many interesting sights, like the deserted Indian village with nineteen elaborate totem poles which Harriman ordered cut down and loaded aboard. The Kodiak bear, object of the journey, was duly killed: a female with a cub at her side was herded into a dead-end gorge near Harriman, who executed her with a single shot and left his underlings the lesser glory of killing her cub.

This accomplished, E. H. wearied of leisure and went back east to get on with wheeling and dealing for his Union Pacific line and his dream of owning a transportation system that would "girdle the earth."

It's hard to imagine – and impossible to calculate – how rich they were, the robber barons of the nineteenth-century railroads. They were so rich that however fast they and their heirs threw money away, it kept on piling up. Newspapers compared their lifestyles to those of Louis XIV, Cleopatra, and Caligula.

They paid no income taxes. They were unburdened by government regulations, public opinion, or charitable, patriotic, or moral concerns. "The public," as William H. Vanderbilt so famously said, "be damned."

Damnation went double for the workers. Jay Gould, lord of ten thousand miles of railway, was asked about the bloody clashes between scab labor and employees who were striking for a guaranteed nine dollars a week. Gould – who made around $100,000 a week – shrugged and said, "I can hire half the working class to kill off the other half."

The railroad barons fiddled with the stocks and either

outfoxed or joined up with one another to build monster monopolies, controlling webs of feeder lines so that a farmer who needed to get his wheat or cattle to market had to pay their price or perish.

They gave secret rebates to major shippers who promised not to use rival lines. They bought congressmen as if they were candy bars and received 180 million acres of public land and government funds beyond measuring. They opened the West, they connected the coasts, they wiped out the Plains Indians. They created towns wherever they stopped or killed them by passing them by. Collis P. Huntington, innovative financier of the Southern Pacific, would ask thriving villages what it was worth to them to have the train come through; if the citizens refused to contribute, the train went elsewhere and grass grew in the streets of the town.

Frank Norris wrote a bitter novel about railroads, calling them (and his book) *The Octopus*. By the 1890s the United States had a third of the rail mileage in the world.

Cornelius ("Commodore") Vanderbilt was the grandaddy of rail barons, best remembered for his remark "What do I care about the law? Hain't I got the power?" The energetic son of poor Staten Island farmers, he started out as a lad ferrying passengers and farm produce over to New York, squeezed out the competition, then raised his rates and prospered. He branched out into steamships and in 1853 took his family to Europe on his yacht, the *North Star*.

She was a marvel. The London *Daily News* gazed on her

270 feet of satinwood, marble, plush, gilded scrollwork, silk and lace berths, and resident caterer, doctor, and chaplain, and gushed, "It is time that the millionaire should cease to be ashamed of having made his fortune. It is time that *parvenu* should be looked on as a word of honor."

Cornelius Vanderbilt was something new under the sun: the unembarrassed flaunter of the fruits of greed. He did well during the Civil War, selling the rotting hulks of his steamships to the federal government and turning his attentions to trains. He quickly mastered the new skills of bribery and speculation and took over the New York and Harlem Railroad. From there his rails spread to Chicago and multiplied until, when he died in 1877, the *New York Herald* called him "the great railway king of the country" and "one of the kings of the earth."

When his wife was reluctant to move to Manhattan, Vanderbilt had her committed to an insane asylum until she changed her mind. He often had his second son committed, too, for gambling and epilepsy. He called his eldest son and heir, William H., a "beetlehead," and sent him off to manage a small farm on Staten Island until William was almost middle-aged.

The Commodore made no pretense of domestic fidelity, literacy, religion, charity, or even legality. He chased the housemaids – and any other young woman who came under his eye – until he was too old to run. Then he took in two sisters, Victoria Woodhull and Tennessee Claflin, who believed in free love and spiritualism; it's said he was specially pleased with their belief in the laying on of hands.

Mark Twain said he'd never read about anything the Commodore had done that he shouldn't be ashamed of, but Vanderbilt died unrepentant at eighty-two. William H., plump and sluggish, came out of the woodwork.

William was just as arrogant as his father, but less fun. He inherited around $100 million and immediately almost doubled it. He was president of the New York Central Railroad in the early 1880s when he said, "I am the richest man in the world. I am worth $194 million. . . . I would not walk across the street to make a million dollars." But apparently he couldn't help himself; at his death several years later the pot was worth more than $200 million.

These were not the pale, tax-ridden, inflation-withered millions of today. These were serious millions, and spending them was serious work.

It was a time of mansions. Jay Gould bought Lyndhurst, a forty-room castle with five hundred acres on the Hudson. Guests at Lyndhurst were rowed out to his yacht, the *Atalanta,* by a crew of ten uniformed sailors. With hospitality like that, even the loathsome Gould could get guests. He was a creepy little fellow, this stock-watering Wall Street whiz kid whose gold-market scam had caused the panic of '69. When he died, the New York *World* departed from its usual obituary style to remark, "Ten thousand ruined men will curse the dead man's memory."

Gould's Lyndhurst was a Gothic fantasy castle from which he commuted by motor launch, but the customary railroad-baronial mansion was on Fifth Avenue, stuffed to the rafters with gilded plaster Cupids, fringes, tassels, curios, and dreadful but expensive paintings. Staircases, ceilings, and whole rooms were transported from Europe and reassembled in Manhattan by European craftsmen. *The New York Times* compared William H. Vanderbilt's house – favorably – to the palaces of "princes and emperors of the Old World" and praised its "Doors of Bronze, Pavements of Mosaic, and Columns of Marble." The inside was decorated by sixty European sculptors imported for the purpose. The stable alone cost six hundred thousand dollars; its courtyard was enclosed in glass so Gould's fancy trotters could exercise in comfort.

William H.'s sons outdid him. Willie K. Vanderbilt's place at Fifty-second and Fifth was a late-Gothic château with a two-storey gym, a Moorish billiards room, and a bathroom cut out of solid marble. Much of the decor, including the salon's carved and gilded wainscotting and the Gobelin tapestries, came from France, where declining aristocratic fortunes were being bolstered by the new American millionaires. Willie's country house on Long Island had a one-hundred-car garage. His brother George created Biltmore in North Carolina, called the grandest private house ever built in America. On its 130,000 acres he employed more men than did the entire U.S. Department of Agriculture. These train lords weren't just rolling in money, like Donald Trump; they were wallowing in it, like Nero.

Another brother, Cornelius II, built the seventy-room cottage called The Breakers at Newport, Rhode Island, where, for a quiet summer evening at home, he imported the first act of a popular Broadway musical, complete with scenery. Entertaining in the Gilded Age was no backyard barbecue.

Willie K. was married to a southern belle named Alva, and Alva was ambitious. She was snubbed by Mrs. Astor, empress of New York society, who apparently found train millions inferior to beaver-skin and real-estate millions. Alva planned a fancy-dress ball that would give Mrs. Astor one in the eye and leave New York talking for decades.

The newspapers babbled hysterically. They likened the party to "the gayest court of Europe," which was just what Alva had in mind – she came as a Venetian princess, her husband as the Duc de Guise, and her brother-in-law Cornelius as Louis XVI. (His wife, more democratically, came as "Electric Light," wearing diamonds enough to blind Broadway.)

The ball opened with the Hobby Horse Quadrille, for which life-size hobby horses, covered with genuine horsehide and draped in embroidered hangings, were attached to the waists of the dancers. The whole party was like that. General Ulysses S. Grant was there; it would be interesting to know what he thought of it.

The Astors were there, too. Socially speaking, the Vanderbilts had arrived, and later were able to buy their daughter, Consuelo, the Duke of Marlborough for $2.5 million down and one hundred thousand dollars a year.

They'd come a long way, the offspring of the ferryboat boy. So had E. H. Harriman, the high-school dropout who came to be in charge of seventy-five thousand miles of track and more men than the U.S. Army. So had Jay Gould, another dropout, and Collis P. Huntington, once a teenage clock peddler, whose private railway car was wondrous to behold. So had Leland Stanford, the hardscrabble farmer's boy who organized the Central Pacific and built a university as a monument to his son.

In those days, you could come all the way by train.

CHICAGO THREW A PARTY

WHEN PRESIDENT GROVER CLEVELAND pressed the button, Chicago's 633-acre World's Columbian Exposition throbbed and glittered with electricity. The orchestra struck up "America the Beautiful," the alabaster city gleamed on cue and, for a moment there, the whole country seemed undimmed by human tears.

It was May 1, 1893, and the party was in honor of the four-hundredth anniversary of Columbus's arrival in the New World. The show was opening a few months late, since time had been lost dickering over the location, but at least the spot had been dedicated on Columbus Day, 1892. To solemnize the dedication and drum up subscriptions, one Francis J. Bellamy, an editor of the magazine *Youth's Companion*, wrote up a pledge of allegiance to the flag, the same one in use today except without the "under God," which was added in 1954. The Federal Bureau of Education sent it around to the schools, all the children stood up to recite it and, presumably, went home to subscribe to *Youth's Companion*. It was a grand time in general for patriotism, confidence, self-congratulation, and advertising.

It was a grand six-month party, too, attended by over twenty-seven million satisfied customers at fifty cents a head. The exhibition palaces that had mushroomed over the winter weren't exactly alabaster, just white plaster smeared over flimsy frames, but their Beaux Arts classic style gave the fairground a feel of ancient Rome crossed with Atlantic City that was much admired and would haunt urban American architecture for decades. Louis Sullivan's award-winning Transportation Building had to be hidden in back because it looked so embarrassingly functional, so American, compared to the Egyptian obelisk or the spire-laden Machinery Hall, a merry mix of classic Greek and Spanish Renaissance.

The Electricity Building, like a great wedding cake frosted with lights, twinkled into the South Canal, where visitors were sculled past in authentic gondolas by authentic gondoliers, bathed in brightness. Edison had come up with the incandescent bulb in 1879, but this was the first time we'd seen what it could do *en masse*. To a mostly rural people used to life by shadowy candlelight and smoky oil lamps, the lightbulbs alone would have been worth the trip. Inspired, Frederick Thompson went back to Coney Island in New York City and strung his Luna Park with a quarter of a million bulbs; his rival, Dreamland, countered with a million. The powers of darkness were on the run.

Inside, the exhibition halls sang hosannas to progress, merchandise, machinery, and the glories of the new century ahead. Facing a new century ourselves, we can only envy

the outrageous optimism; we will never again be so innocent, so hopeful, so cocky.

The Electricity Building held, in addition to the first
working electric locomotive, a model home bristling with
electric stoves, hot plates, washing machines, doorbells,
carpet sweepers, and other new desirables. The Manufacturers and Liberal Arts Building dangled forty-four acres of
ownable goodies before the great American middle class.
Well-lighted products, from the first commemorative
stamps and coins to Jell-O, baby carriages, phonographs,
telephones, lawn furniture, and zippers, radiated entice-
ment. Shredded Wheat and Cream of Wheat, Aunt Jemima
pancake mix, and Juicy Fruit gum made dazzling debuts.
People previously more accustomed to producing than consuming suddenly realized that the Good Life didn't have to
be made; it could be bought and carried home in a box.

Not that all was crass materialism. The World's Parlia-
ment of Religions convened at the Fair and must have had
an unusually jolly time. High-minded seminars were held.
John Dewey spoke on education, Samuel Gompers on labor, and Julia Ward Howe on women. The intellectual curmudgeon Henry Adams came twice and spent days and
days brooding darkly on the steam engines and dynamos.
Later he wrote about them at length; he felt that they
meant religion was dead and civilization as he'd known it
was but a road kill on the path of progress. The Fair's
architecture, he added, was designed to appeal to "the superstitious and ignorant savage within us." He was deeply
depressed. Adamses have never been your ideal fairgoers.

For uplift, there was a $5 million art exhibit. For instruction, the Women's Building gave cooking and child-care lessons, and the Fisheries set up aquaria displaying marine wonders from sharks to catfish. You could, in short, spend several busy, educational days at the Fair without ever sampling the Midway Plaisance, the Ferris wheel or, just outside the gates, Buffalo Bill's Wild West.

Not many visitors deprived themselves, though, and even Henry Adams hit the Midway in order to come back and call it "fakes and frauds."

He may have meant the medium Minnie Williams who, ably assisted by two gorillas, passed along messages from notables like Aristotle, Jesus, and Henry Ward Beecher. Or he may have meant the young Harry Houdini, who saw a fellow magician there doing the Handcuff Trick, mastered it, and promptly set himself up as "Handcuff King and Escape Artist."

The Midway was a mile-long entertainment strip to the west of the serious fair, marked by George Ferris's 264-foot wheel, invented for the occasion. For fifty cents you could ride around twice in a glass car that held sixty people – 2,160 people revolved at once, admiring the view of the fairgrounds. (Several couples begged in vain to be married at the top.) Within a decade the Ferris wheel was standard equipment at every amusement park in the country, though rarely on such a dramatic scale.

After the wheel, you could rise up fifteen hundred feet in a captive balloon; ride several kinds of railroads; hire a chair and be rolled in state past the Hawaiian volcano, the Turkish bazaar, the circus animals, and heavyweight champ Jim Corbett; or gawk at those less civilized and less white than yourself, all in the name of education.

In these politically incorrect times, there was nothing like a good "ethnological display," where Americans could giggle at the weird ways of the rest of the world. Civilization was smugly laid out in a kind of descending order, beginning with Teutonic and Celtic displays and sliding downhill past Asian and Moslem exhibits toward the flat-out savages.

The Middle East was represented by Cairo Street, where fully clad belly dancers gyrated. One fairgoer observed that they were "homely as owls" but had sexy feet; their feet, unlike their bellies, were bare. The exhibit's popularity spawned the generations of "girlie" sideshows that gave many a country boy his first lesson in female anatomy.

At the bottom of the scale was a group of "cannibals" imported from West Africa for the occasion. While they weren't seen actually eating people, they did sit around looking satisfied, as if remembering lunch. (By summer they were clamoring for Pabst beer, the Fair's blue-ribbon winner; no doubt a mug of Pabst goes well with anyone.)

Outside the gates a separate show was packing them in. As the *Chicago News* put it, "No other exhibition has received the plaudits of the people as has Buffalo Bill's Wild West."

It wasn't officially part of the Fair. Because it involved a cast of five or six hundred, including genuine Indians, Arabs, Cossacks, and the cavalry of four armies, all camped out on the premises, the Fair officials felt it would be a jarring note among the pleasure domes and Greek pillars.

Undaunted, Colonel "Buffalo Bill" Cody leased fifteen acres across from the Fair's entrance, where he built a grandstand to seat eighteen thousand.

Opening nearly a month ahead of the Fair itself, "Buffalo Bill's Wild West and Congress of Rough Riders of the World" was an instant smash. The Illinois Central extended its Fair train and the El built a new station to accommodate its twenty-five thousand daily visitors.

Two shows a day, seven days a week, featured The Indian Encampment, The Pony Express, spine-tingling reenactments of The Attack on Deadwood Stage, and feats of horsemanship that inspired little boys to go home and risk their necks on poor old Dobbin. Between shows the grounds alone, with cast encamped, were worth the price of admission, along with the chance of meeting the hero himself, crusted with gold lace and telling tall tales. He wasn't part of the show, but he came close to stealing it.

America fell in love with itself at the Fair. It was everyone's fair. Philadelphia's Centennial party in 1876 had been subdued by the local blue laws: it closed on Sundays. It also closed at six in the evening, for fear of fires from the gas lighting. This effectively kept out the working folk, who couldn't get there before six and had only Sundays off. By contrast, open seven days a week, glittering with flameless electric lights by night, the Chicago Fair opened its arms. Everyone could come, and nearly everyone did.

It was the best of Fairs: it was the worst of times. Five days after the grand opening, the stock market plunged. Presently more than twelve thousand businesses had failed, six hundred banks closed, and Coxey's Army marched on

Washington demanding relief for the unemployed. All that progress and prosperity celebrated at the Fair was as precarious as its flimsy plaster buildings.

But when times are good who needs a fabulous fair? What's a fair for, after all?

GRAND OLD GIRLY SHOW

ON THE GREAT DAY IN 1944 when Paris was liberated, according to French legend, the first words of the first GI marching in were "Oo way lay Follies Burr Jayer, sill voo play?"

It might even be true. For 123 years the Folies-Bergère has drawn foreign tourists like ants to a picnic, and half the tongues of the earth are spoken in its lounge and bar, with the possible exception of French. This polyglot crowd has always shaped the offerings; they're not aural, but visual – grandly, overwhelmingly, splendidly visual – and the gags are sight gags or easily understood from props and gestures. Send the sophisticate to the Comédie Française, the snob to the Louvre, and give the rest of the world what it wants, girls and gorgeousness that vault the language barrier.

Here Josephine Baker, America's "Black Pearl," stormed on stage wearing a girdle of bananas and brought the world to its feet. Here a thin sulky boy named Charles Chaplin, barely twenty but already a veteran actor, played a buffoon in an oversized frock coat that inked in the outline of his future. Here Colette, who later became the first lady of French literature, danced and mimed and entranced the audience with what her partner called "the most exciting, appetizing bosom in the world!"

That partner was Maurice Chevalier, Mr. Debonair to several generations, who also danced with Mistinguett, or "Miss," as she was fondly named. If Colette's was the best bosom, Miss had the best legs, insured for one hundred thousand World War I dollars. The great sculptor Rodin said that if he were to attempt the "Muse of the Music Hall," she'd have Miss's legs. At the Folies-Bergère she and Chevalier did a skit that opened with a ferocious quarrel, during which she slapped him thirty times and they threw all the props and furniture into the wings. Then they whirled into a frenzied waltz that showed plenty of the famous legs, collapsed in each other's arms, rolled themselves up in the carpet, and vanished offstage. They spent a good deal of time wrapped in that carpet together and presently fell in love; their stormy romance blazed for many years.

The oldest music hall in Paris, the Folies-Bergère opened on May Day, 1869, twenty years before its rowdy sister, the Moulin Rouge. It offered a varied menu – acrobats, dancing girls, jugglers, a woman with two heads, wrestlers, clowns, mimes, animal acts, and a magician who, for his finale, ripped open his stomach and pulled out pearl necklaces to present to the ladies. Another early hit was Le Pétomane, a gentleman in impeccable white tie and tails who produced recognizable tunes by purely intestinal means. Nudes were yet to come. The thrill of the cancan, popular since the 1840s, was the high kick revealing a flash of flesh between the black stockings and the foaming ruffles, well worth crossing the Channel, or even the Atlantic, to glimpse.

If in the beginning the dancers remained respectable, at least on stage, the ladies of the *promenoir* never pretended to be. The *promenoir,* or strolling area, was behind the orchestra seats in what we call standing room, and the working girls who'd been waiting on the cold hard sidewalk to pick up their overstimulated customers after the show relocated into its warmth and comfort. The Folies-Bergère became a world-famous place to look for love. Owner-manager Paul Derval, who took over in 1916, struggled for decades to preserve a certain restraint among its peddlers, issuing identity cards only to those who behaved themselves and dressed decorously. Long before his time, though, the ladies on stage were dressing less and less decorously.

The first resounding crack in the dress code came at midnight on February 9, 1893, not at the Folies-Bergère but at the Moulin Rouge, rented by the Beaux-Arts students for their traditional exuberant arts ball. All the artists' models in Paris were there, and a controversy arose among them over who had the prettiest legs. Legs were compared and judged. The girls hopped onto the tables, shoulders were exposed and considered, then bosoms. Finally a spirited lass named Mona sprang up to offer her entire self in competition, drawing an ovation from the assembled students.

The matter reached the ear of a Senator Béranger, known

as Papa Prudery, and he hauled Mona and a sampling of students into court. The judge let them off with a hundred-franc fine and a suspended sentence, but even that was too much for the Latin Quarter, and the students rioted. The police charged into them, and a young man in a café was fatally wounded; in response the students laid siege to police headquarters. Troops were called in. The fracas was finally resolved with the dismissal of the prefect of police, but the excitement brought on by Mona's exposure had riveted the attention of the entertainment world: this undressing thing had possibilities.

Total nakedness, under the eye of Papa Prudery, was out of the question, but that was circumvented by the invention of the striptease, or gradual and not-quite-complete exposure, ingeniously dramatized in some wondrous skits. The titles of hits like "Suzanne and the Heat Wave" and "Liane at the Doctor's" speak for themselves. In one smash that toured all Europe, "The Flea," the heroine pursued the offending insect around her anatomy to varying extents, depending on local laws. Almost overnight, undressing became a major art form.

The Folies-Bergère strove to go bare more tastefully. Flesh-colored tights, easily transformed into flesh by the eye of the overheated spectator, were an option; the Spanish dancer La Belle Otéro did famous justice to hers. Elaborate romantic playlets involving gods and goddesses, historical events, exotic settings, and filmy scarves preserved the notion that this was, as the visiting Englishman could tell his wife, not sex but art. The authorities were backed down, literally inch by inch, until the only essential garment shrank to a tiny, almost invisible triangle of fabric held in place by spirit gum.

Jugglers, performing dogs, and expensive star dancers were gradually edged offstage by troupes of nudes, only a few of whom could do much more than walk on and strike a pose. Early in the twentieth century, Colette perched backstage between scenes and caught them in her notebooks for *La Vagabonde* and *L'Envers du Music Hall*. While the audiences cheered for the gorgeous spectacle out front, she wrote about icy drafts and suffocating heat; about trailing exhausted through the provinces on tour; about undernourished little chorus girls, half dead for sleep, rubbing their chilblains or hunched over darning a baby's sock. (There were always babies, some suckled and raised backstage, their mothers cherishing a cynical, melancholy independence of men.)

Except for a star like Mistinguett, it wasn't a glamorous life, but it was always a glamorous show. Its descendants proliferated on our own shores, from the seedy strip joints of *Gypsy* to the glittering productions of Flo Ziegfeld and the high-kicking lines of Rockettes.

As another turn of the century looms, visitors to Paris still report in to the Folies-Bergère, some perhaps in a genuine lust for bare bosoms – though it's hard to see how such a thirst could have gone unslaked in today's world – and some for nostalgia's sake. Sophisticated guidebooks speak a bit scornfully of the landmark and tend to mention Las Vegas, but who, after all, was Las Vegas's great-grandmother? Who taught her everything she knows?

WHERE THE ENGLISH LEFT THEIR HEARTS

FOR THREE AND A HALF centuries, from the days of Good Queen Bess until after World War II, Englishmen went to work in India. In commercial, civil, diplomatic, or military jobs, most of them worked hard and honestly – and struggled to hold onto their Englishness against the seductions of a magically tempting world.

It was, to modern eyes, a curious relationship. In 1600 Queen Elizabeth I chartered the East India Company, always to be called simply "the Company," holding a monopoly in trade with the East. But India had never been a single country, and dealing with its many rulers was a frustrating, piecemeal business. There was no written law, only the whims of the rajas; famines and religious wars were usual; the peasants struggled to survive on leftovers from drought and taxes. The remnants of the Mogul Empire – Hindu conquerors who had swept down from the north in the previous century – had decayed into isolated feudal kingdoms.

At first the Company went begging for scraps of coastal

land where they could set up warehouses and trading stations. Moguls whose tributes and tax collections had made them considerably richer than Queen Elizabeth hadn't much interest in commerce, but neither were they interested in government as we know it. The Company bought some land, paid tribute on some, and some they were simply given. Hundreds of principalities, from tiny to twice the size of Pennsylvania, agreed to the status of "protected states," with rulers still enjoying their emeralds, wives, and elephants while the Company did all the boring work of governing.

Piece by piece through the seventeenth century, the princes handed over responsibilities like tax collection and peace-keeping to the Company. Merchants who had come to trade in ginger, sugar, woolen goods, opium, diamonds, cotton, indigo, and vermilion found themselves in the odd position of administrators. On top of the paperwork, they were expected to be able to lead a company of infantry, doctor the sick, lay out a road, design public buildings, and act as policemen.

Being English, they rolled up their sleeves and set about trying to create an English world under the Indian sun. To them, an English world meant internal peace, written laws, justice, payable taxes, maps, roads, bridges, railways, canals, irrigation, sanitation, dispensaries, reservoirs, fair play, and an orderly life. It was hard work in a country that had never known any of these, but – being English – they saw it as their duty.

And they fell in love. They loved the space, the light, the smells, the adventures, the early morning horseback rides.

They loved the work they saw as useful. Far from their cramped and foggy little island, many of them refused to take their home leaves. They stayed for decades. They stayed for generations.

It can be argued that all foreign domination is tyranny, but the staggering majority of Indians had never known anything else and found English tyranny a great relief after the previous examples. How do twelve hundred civilians with fifty thousand soldiers govern 300 million people in a country the size of Europe? Gently. Carefully. To a country accustomed to rigid castes, the English simply added another caste: themselves.

From the beginning, social life with the Indians was constricted by taboos. To a Hindu, Westerners were untouchable and it was defilement to eat in their company; food over which their shadows had fallen was contaminated. Muslims could eat no pork, or any meat that might have been killed by a non-Muslim; Hindus could eat no beef. Many Buddhists were strict vegetarians. A Sikh could drink with a European but not smoke; a Muslim could smoke but not drink. Most women couldn't socialize at all. Who could entertain such neighbors?

But in spite of restrictions, in the eighteenth century it was usual enough for an Englishman to keep an Indian mistress and lead, as far as possible, an almost Indian life. No stigma was attached to wearing comfortable Indian clothes, eating Indian food, and smoking a hookah. Marriageable English women were scarce; the trip out took months and the climate was considered deadly. Besides, marriage was looked on as a drawback, a distraction from work, and a restraint on courageous soldiering.

A joyously masculine world evolved. In the provinces, the district officer rode out every morning at dawn and saw his people, settled disputes, investigated crimes, shot a marauding tiger, inspected the crops, and oversaw his pet projects, his tree plantings, or his irrigation ditches. In the cantonments, soldiers drilled in stiff, heavy British uniforms; the sepoys – native troops – learned the strange customs of British discipline and took great pride in them. In the cities, civilians went for a dawn gallop and then worked from seven until four – long hours for a hot country. After work, there was sport. Polo for the cavalry; hockey for the infantry; pig-sticking, hunting, shooting, and cricket for everyone. Then dinner and the club for bridge, billiards, gossip. And early to bed. For those who dodged the endemic dysentery, cholera, and malaria, it was a healthy life.

And always there was the strange and alluring land around them. Contemporaries suggested that the British in India hedged themselves in with English sports, games, and habits in self-defense, to block out the siren song of the country. You can hear the song in Kipling; hear his terrible urge to let go of his Englishness and give himself over utterly to the land of his heart. The English saw this temptation as a kind of original sin and wrestled mightily against it.

In 1869 the Suez Canal cut four thousand miles off the trip from England, and India was suddenly flooded with marriageable women, known as "the Fishing Fleet." They came, they saw, they conquered. Married, the English gave up their Indian mistresses and put on proper clothes. Curries were replaced by muffins and marmalade, respectability settled in like London fog, and relations with the Indians suffered. The British grew starchy and self-important, conscious of their civilizing role. Missionaries threatened the precarious balance of religions.

And for the English brides, life was never as much fun as it was for their husbands. Very few defied convention to take an interest in the culture around them, which they saw as a threat to propriety. With no useful work to do, they spent their days entangled in what must have been a bewildering web of servants.

An ordinary household might have sixty or seventy in help, less from ostentation than from a network of customs more complicated than a dozen labor unions. The sweeper and his assistants were "untouchables" and could only sweep the patio and empty the commodes, while the butler was so lofty his duty was simply to stand behind the master's chair at dinner. The cook needed a coolie to carry groceries home from the bazaar, a boy to carry them from pantry to kitchen, and still more assistants to scrub the pots. The washerman could only wash; the dog boy could only brush and walk the dog.

And the unfortunate *memsahib* could only read the illustrated London papers at the club. During the hot season she was sent like a parcel to one of the cool hill stations, where she could gossip with other wives or, with luck, flirt with young officers. As late as 1931, Vere Ogilvie, the seventh generation of her family to live in India, found the life "excessively boring, trivial, claustrophobic, confined, and totally male-oriented."

Women didn't even have children to raise. The offspring of foot soldiers could stay, glorying in dust and sunshine and the acquaintance of camel drivers, but middle-class children past the age of five were sent away to live with relatives they had probably never seen, in a place their parents mysteriously called "home." This was partly for their health, partly for their education, and partly to make sure they grew up truly English, untainted by the siren song.

Some never saw their families again. Readers of children's classics may think of India as an orphan maker: in *The Secret Garden,* Frances Hodgson Burnett orphans her heroine with a stroke of cholera that wipes out her parents and a houseful of servants overnight; in *A Little Princess,* her heroine's father dies in Bombay of jungle fever. Kipling's young Kim, a soldier's son, loses his mother to cholera and his father to opium and drink, and wanders happily through the bazaars and countryside until England reclaims him.

In England the children, like Jon and Rumer Godden in their memoir, *Two Under the Indian Sun,* remembered their childhood as dusted all over with gold, blooming with friendly people, with animals, with excitement, and a happiness almost too brilliant to be true. Kipling himself was sent to England at six, and perhaps reappears in his story "Baa Baa, Black Sheep" as the little boy Punch, who in homesick misery tries to kill himself. As soon as school released him, Kipling returned to India.

India called her English children back. They came back as subalterns, as wives, as bureaucrats at desks or district officers on horseback, as diplomats dealing with native princes or engineers designing dams. However pompous and intolerant some of them were, India still sang in their hearts.

The English had always intended to leave, eventually. They'd always called themselves stewards; always planned to turn over the reins to the Indians when the Indians were ready to hold them. With this in mind, they'd set up English-style schools, examination systems, congress, and training programs; they brought the Indians into civil and military positions with at least limited authority.

In the end, though, it caught them off balance. It happened faster than they'd expected. Or perhaps they'd never quite realized they'd actually have to pack and go away.

They left behind, along with two million British graves, much of the light and joy of their lives. One young man, headed "home" in 1947, wrote, "though I felt it my duty to leave India, I shall never cease to yearn for another glimpse of a land that gave me so much happiness."

THE FREEMASON GUESSING GAME

RUDYARD KIPLING WROTE the story a hundred years ago and Sean Connery and Michael Caine starred in the swashbuckler "The Man Who Would Be King." Two wandering English scoundrels set forth to seek their fortune in the remote, icy mountains of Kafiristan, among famously bloodthirsty tribes. Kipling, being a brother Mason, helps them on their way as a brother must. In the movie version, as the high priest prepares to poke a spear into the Connery character, he sees a Masonic medallion on the bared chest, cries out, and the whole population falls down in awe. They recognize the symbol as the sign of Alexander the Great, who came to these mountains and left a king's ransom in jewels, promising to send his son to claim it one of these days. For two thousand years they've been guarding the treasure and waiting; now here at last is the son. For a brief, giddy time, a couple of million people in mountains remote as the moon revere the English rascal as god, king, and Alexander II.

Powerful stuff, Freemasonry.

The Ancient Order of Free and Accepted Masons is the world's most successful secret society and object of more furious papal bulls and encyclicals than any other. Until 1717, when four Lodges in London banded together and met openly as a Grand Lodge, it was secret indeed. So secret that its history has been lost to even its inmost authorities. In 1986 John Hamill, librarian and curator of the United Grand Lodge Library and Museum in London, in his book, "The Craft," asks when, why, and where Freemasonry was born, and answers himself, "We do not know. . . . Whether we shall ever discover the true origins of Freemasonry is open to question."

Most modern Masons and standard reference books subscribe to the current theory that it grew from a medieval craft guild of stonemasons, but on closer inspection this seems unlikely. Earlier Masonic historians included Adam, Abraham, Noah, Moses, Ptolemy, Julius Caesar, and the mythical Achilles as members. The murder of Hiram, master builder of the Temple of Solomon, is central to its highest rites, and King Solomon is held to have been one of the three original Grand Masters. Speculation has also linked it to every heretical sect; to the Holy Grail, the KGB, devil worship, Wat Tyler's bloody Peasants' Revolt in 1381, the Protestant Reformation, ancient Egyptian priests, the Crusades, the Rosicrucians, the Jacobites, and the Druids.

Odd as it would seem for a craft guild of dusty stonecutters, the order has traditionally contained kings and dukes, scientists, writers, and other notables. The Royal Society in London, still one of the world's most prestigious gatherings, was founded around 1645 by England's foremost scientists and philosophers; virtually all of them were Masons. The Stuart kings were heavily involved, and Prince Charles is the first male British heir in two hundred years to opt out. Voltaire and Goethe, Benjamin Franklin, Alexander Hamilton, the Marquis de Lafayette, Sir Walter Scott, and Mark Twain were Masons.

The reference books explain this distinguished roster with the theory that, as the numbers of working stonemasons dwindled, outsiders were allowed to join. This is like saying that the dockworkers' union, finding itself short-handed, let the king of England sign up.

In America, where the order is almost three million strong, fifteen presidents, from George Washington to Ronald Reagan, have been Masons. John Quincy Adams, however, raged wildly against the society, and President Fillmore got his start in politics on the third-party Anti-Masonic ticket.

Secrets – and the implications of a worldwide underground of influential people pledged to help and protect each other – inspire paranoia in outsiders. We consider uneasily the Masonic mark on our dollar bill, the All-Seeing Eye and the unfinished pyramid symbolizing the Temple of Solomon that Masons swear to complete. What voodoo lurks behind the buck? A popular book of 1976, Stephen Knight's *Jack the Ripper – The Final Solution,* accused prominent Freemasons of Jack's gory mutilations.

As with all mysteries, theories have multiplied like rabbits. One particularly tireless researcher, John J. Robinson, has worked out a plausible link between Freemasory and the Knights Templar, who were outlawed in the fourteenth century. In his book, *Born in Blood – The Lost Secrets of*

Freemasonry, he makes short work of the stonemason idea. For starters, he can't find any mention of medieval masons' guilds at all, even in towns like Oxford and Lincoln, with mountains of stonework and exhaustive records. And most precious to the Masonic rites is the apron, originally lamb-skin, supposedly the working uniform of a stonecutter, yet no contemporary drawing or woodcut shows builders wearing aprons. The accepted origin of Masonic "Lodges" as temporary work-site quarters looks doubtful, too, considering that a medieval castle or cathedral could take from twenty to one hundred years to build – a long time to be camped out away from the wife and kiddies.

The hair-raising oaths, the blindfolds, the guard at the Lodge door with his sword drawn, seem extreme for a craft guild. What secrets were such desperate matters – a new way to hold a chisel or swing a maul? Until 1717 even membership was a close-held secret, not to be revealed to any except an identified brother, but secrecy would have made a guild worker helpless to apply for a job or travel to one from town to town, since medieval movements were fiercely restricted and the penalty for vagrancy could be death. A stonemason on his way to work would need to explain himself at every checkpoint.

In the old order of Masonry there are three degrees, Entered Apprentice, Fellow Craft, and Master Mason, each with its separate initiation, oath, and separately revealed secrets. An Apprentice swears that if he breaks secrecy or endangers a brother Mason, he accepts the penalty of "having my throat cut across, my tongue torn out by its roots, and my body buried in the rough sands of the sea, at low-water mark . . ." At the Fellow Craft rites, he swears to aid all Fellow Crafts and their widows and orphans or "have my left breast torn open and my heart and vitals taken from thence and thrown over my left shoulder and carried into the valley of Jehosaphat . . ." Advancing to Master Mason, he asks that his body be cut in two and his bowels burned to ashes if he breaks his oath of secrecy.

Strong words for a labor union. At all levels secret grips, passwords, and interrogations are doled out, and all swear to lodge a traveling brother for two weeks before giving him money to continue his journey.

Robinson makes a good case for a group of fugitives in danger of death, possibly by official torture, being passed from safe house to safe house by strangers in whom the outlaw must trust absolutely, by reason of their oaths. He believes that at least the original core members were the Knights Templar. Perhaps they used stonework and its symbols as a cover, the way outlawed early Christians called themselves fishermen and used the sign of the fish.

Founded after the First Crusade in 1118 as a standing army in the Holy Land, the Templars were a religious body of warrior monks who wore lambskin underpants as a reminder of their vows of chastity and identified themselves with the Temple of Solomon. There were three ranks. They convened in secret, and a knight guarded the door with drawn sword.

They belonged to the knightly, not the artisan, social class and had lands and connections all over Europe. Their ranks swelled to fifteen thousand and, as they got richer, they took up banking, developed a secret intelligence system, and lent money to Philip IV of France. As others have discovered, it's risky to let powerful people get deep in your debt.

Pope Clement V was a tool of Philip's and between them they developed a classic frame-up. One "prisoner" confessed to another that he was a Templar and that Templars were devoted to heresy, blasphemy, sodomy, and worshiping a cat. Both prisoners were plants. The pope, directed by Philip, ordered the Templars arrested on Friday the 13th, 1307, and tortured by having their feet burned off and their leg bones slowly crushed until they confessed.

Mysteriously, many vanished into the woodwork, taking along sacks of money and eighteen ships that were never seen again – unless, perhaps, flying the Masonic skull and crossbones.

In Britain the pope had less clout; Scotland simply ignored the order, and Edward II in England procrastinated until Clement personally sent ten of his best torturers. Great numbers of Templars remained unfound.

They were French-speakers, and as outlaws among English-speakers they would need hand signs and grips to communicate. Robinson has traced many of the unaccountable Masonic words to medieval French, corrupted by the English-speakers. Maybe the "due-guard," for instance, the sign by which a Mason identifies himself, comes from "*geste du garde,*" or protective gesture.

Or then again, maybe not. And maybe, like the common cold, Freemasonry has many sources. None of what Robinson offers is documentary evidence, but where there's no evidence for anyone's theory, anyone can join in. The history of Freemasonry, like the Kennedy assassination, provides an endless playground for buffs who love a mystery.

Laughing All the Way

Q: Who first said, "All the things I really like to do are either illegal, immoral, or fattening"? A: Alexander Woollcott, the theater critic known to his friends as the Butcher of Broadway and to the rest of us as Kaufman and Hart's irascible *Man Who Came to Dinner*. He said it, among other *bons mots*, over lunch at the Algonquin Hotel.

Who first said, "Let's get out of these wet clothes and into a dry martini"? Writer and comedian Robert Benchley, coming out of the rain through the Algonquin's glass-and-brass doors, on his way to lunch with Woollcott, and Dorothy Parker, and Marc (*Green Pastures*) Connelly, and Harold Ross, founding father of *The New Yorker,* and columnist Franklin P. Adams, and playwrights Robert Sherwood, George S. Kaufman, and Edna (*Show Boat*) Ferber.

Lunch went on for ten years. Sooner or later almost everyone we've heard of from the twenties sat at the famous table. Actors, playwrights, musicians, critics, editors, cartoonists, poets, and painters crowded around. Frank

Case, the owner, moved them to the Rose Room and gave them the enormous round table, with its own waiter, that became center stage for an era. A Broadway press agent christened the Algonquinians the Round Table, as in King Arthur's knights of Camelot. (Others, stung by their homicidal humor, called it the Vicious Circle.)

In those days New York was where you had to be, where fame and fortune waited. You packed up your talent and a change of socks and headed for Manhattan, because Hollywood was still a cultural branch office and the rest of the country might as well have been Mars, fame-and-fortune-wise. New York was the center of the talent universe, and the Algonquin was the center of New York.

The Algonquin was, and is, a twelve-storey hotel on West Forty-fourth Street, near Fifth Avenue, ordinary enough to the eye but strangely appealing to the arts and entertainment world as far back as Mark Twain. It was planned, in 1902, as a temperance hotel to be called The Puritan, both concepts that were scrapped with awesome thoroughness.

Here, in 1919, lunched three merry, wicked young friends still tenuously employed by the original *Vanity Fair* magazine – Benchley, Sherwood, and the rapier-wielding poet Dorothy Parker. They called it the Gonk. Being poor, they ate whatever food was set out free, ordered the scrambled eggs, and sat for hours making each other laugh. The plump and waspish Woollcott joined them, then Kaufman, then Adams, who had published Parker's first poems in his column "The Conning Tower" in *The New York World*.

Their laughter echoed beyond the walls of the hotel. Adams reported their high jinks in his column; other journalists hung around listening, and today's wisecracks brightened tomorrow's papers until the group grew more famous for its wit than its work. Tidbits, such as Parker's comment on men's passes and girls who wear glasses, worked their way into the language. (Alas, many of her best cracks have been lost to history because they were unprintable, though uttered in her low, sweet voice and accompanied by what James Thurber called "the eloquent magic of her dark and lovely eyes.")

The lunchers punctured the pompous and teased the establishment, but they loved each other dearly. They were young, they were funny, they were talented and light-hearted and happy together in a way that now seems, sadly, to belong to a long-ago world. Their merriment and affection were magnetic, and the group expanded.

Sometimes lunch lasted till the small hours of the next morning. On Saturday nights the Round Table moved upstairs and became the Thanatopsis Literary and Inside Straight Club, playing poker till dawn and sometimes till Monday. (Harpo Marx won the most, Woollcott lost the hardest.) The core of the group grew more and more dependent on each other's company and began spending all their time together. "But don't they ever see anyone bloody else?" asked Noël Coward in wonder. "We just hated being apart," said Marc Connelly. When forced asunder, they suffered from separation anxiety and stayed in touch by telegram. Suburban married members took rooms at the Gonk and saw less and less of their families.

Afternoons between four and seven usually found them at the studio of portraitist Neysa McMein who, in a concession to Prohibition, had a still in her bathroom that pumped out rivers of reliable drink. Here the Algonquin regulars could catch up with fringe members like Charlie Chaplain, Ethel Barrymore, Paul Robeson, George Gershwin, and Irving Berlin. Later they might go on to Tony's, their favorite speakeasy, or pick up some money reviewing a new play. Broadway was bustling: 256 new productions opened in 1924, sometimes half a dozen on the same night, and most of the group did stints of reviewing from time to time. It was Parker who wrote, of a forgettable play called *The Lake,* that Katharine Hepburn "ran the emotional gamut from A to B." And Parker again, reviewing books as "Constant Reader" for *The New Yorker,* who slammed A. A. Milne's *The House at Pooh Corner* with "Tonstant Weader fwowed up."

Late at night they gathered at the house of Polly Adler, the world's most famous madam, until the sun came up and it was time for bed. And always they talked. Half the day and all night long they entertained themselves and each other with words. "Conversation was like oxygen to us," said Connelly. They batted each other's opinions around, traded insults, argued, and cracked each other up. They played a game based on the schoolteachers' "use-this-word-in-a-sentence" test. Samples: Horticulture – "You can lead a horticulture but you can't make her think" (Parker). Punctilious – "I know a farmer who has two daughters, Lizzie and Tillie. Lizzie's all right but you wouldn't believe how punctilious" (Kaufman).

In summer they retreated to Woollcott's place on Long Island, which was famous for compulsory croquet. Here romances bloomed and faded; here Harpo sometimes popped out of the bushes wearing nothing but a straw hat.

In the magical summer of 1926, immortalized in F. Scott Fitzgerald's *Tender is the Night,* they all went to the French Riviera to frolic with the Gerald Murphys. Soft-hearted Parker didn't enjoy the Pamplona trip and Hemingway's bulls, and Rudolph Valentino felt ill, left early, and went back to New York to die, plunging the world into mourning. Otherwise it was very like heaven, that "summer of a thousand parties." (Except, we suppose, for the hangovers.) Then back to the Gonk, and to work.

When did they work? It's true that many of their biographies outweigh the subjects' songs, stories, drawings, essays, verses, and plays, but what they did produce is brilliantly crafted, carefully polished, the sort of work that needs time, privacy, and a clear head, all of which must have been in short supply.

The most productive writers of the era – Hemingway, Faulkner, Steinbeck, O'Hara – stayed on the fringes, partying with the Round Table but never committed to talking eighteen hours a day. (Still, they were close enough to catch the infection; when Faulkner won the Nobel Prize for Literature, Steinbeck wired him "Joyeux Nobel.")

If the work the Round Table left shows glittering talent, having produced it under the circumstances shows downright genius. Edna Ferber said, "Theirs was a tonic influence, one on the other, and on the world of American letters." Perhaps if there'd been less gin in the tonic, total production would have been higher, but let us be grateful for what we have.

By 1930 the movies were talking and Hollywood was suddenly starved for writers, coaxing them to the coast with seductive salaries. The Vicious Circle gradually shifted its center of gravity from the Algonquin to bungalows at the flaky "Garden of Allah" complex, where Tallulah Bankhead strolled the grounds in the nude. The parties went on, with the Californian addition of swimming pools into which everyone jumped, wearing either all or none of their clothes.

Just the same, the golden years of laughter were winding down. The Depression, the war in Spain, and the rise of Hitler politicized some of the group, forging such unlikely new friendships as Dorothy Parker's with Lillian Hellman. The old bonds held, but the new world seemed much less funny. There were no more snowball fights on West Forty-fourth Street, no more dashes to Greenwich Village to get tattooed. Never again would Parker, too broke to pay her hotel bill, call an ambulance and have herself carried out past the front desk on a stretcher.

As the sign over "Bedlam Bob" Benchley's desk said, "The work can wait." The Round Table believed that having fun was the best way to spend the time, taking oneself seriously was the only cardinal sin, and laughter was a goal worth any effort.

No wonder, in these earnest days, we look back on the lighthearted crew a bit wistfully. No wonder some of us, when in New York, drop by the Algonquin for a commemorative – though legal – drink, and strain to hear the laughter of the joyful ghosts.

When Glamor Rode the Train

FOR NINETY YEARS it connected the capitals of Europe across fifteen hundred miles. With a link to London, it ran from Paris to Constantinople, gateway to the mysterious East. It was the playground of the rich and powerful and, for those who could afford it, the only way to go.

The word "glamor" has been abused almost to extinction, but if it still means anything it ought to mean opulence, drama, exotic travel, a glimpse of royalty, and the chance to share a bottle of bubbly with a beautiful spy. Glamor ought to mean the Orient Express. Jingling with silver and crystal at six-course, six-wine meals, it carried the Empress Elizabeth and Crown Prince Rudolph, the Duke of Windsor and Mrs. Simpson, the Aga Khan, the Maharajah of Cutch-Behar, Sarah Bernhardt, Harry Houdini, Mata Hari, Mahler, Strauss, Diaghilev, Toscanini. All of them woke up daily to the tap of a conductor who could say "good morning" in any traveler's native tongue.

European royalty treated it as their own. They used it to join or escape from or banish their mistresses, to go into or return from exile, to slip off for unpublicized vacations or negotiations with other rulers. Prince Boris of Bulgaria loved driving it. The minute it crossed the border into his country he pulled the emergency brake, climbed into the cab, and exercised his royal prerogative by taking the controls. His driving style could be described as "reckless endangerment," but a prince is, in his own land, a prince.

When King Carol of Romania was exiled in 1940 he boarded the train with only the barest necessities – his mistress Magda Lupesco, two hundred suitcases, and booty from the palace that stuffed two saloon cars and a sleeping car. King Leopold II of Belgium found it discreet to lodge his mistress, the dancer Cleo de Merode, in his private car attached to the train. (It wasn't discreet enough. Jokers took to calling him "King Cleopold.")

A train, of course, is not a single vessel like a ship. It's made of detachable parts that may be sent off on assignment anywhere in the company's far-flung network. Its routes change as tracks are laid, destinations added or canceled, bridges built or tunnels dug, wars fought and borders altered. The Orient Express traveled various routes and evolved through many changes, but it stood for glamor always.

The idea was born in 1869 when a Belgian named Georges Nagelmackers, visiting the United States, admired the elegant Pullman cars and determined to start an international luxury railroad across Europe. It was a daunting challenge. Quarrelsome countries had built their railroad tracks to be incompatible with their neighbors' to discourage invasions. Each Balkan state had to be separately persuaded. And the suggested journey, from Paris to Constantinople, was long indeed.

A breakthrough came with the creation of the first restaurant car, in Munich, sporting an impeccable wine list, walls padded in Spanish leather, and painted Italian ceilings. A train that served meals could run straight through without pausing at way stations for passengers to forage food on the platforms. This cut a day and a half off Nagelmackers's proposed route, and suddenly the funding, spearheaded by King Leopold, began to flow in.

Service began in 1883. Cheered and feted and serenaded along the way, the varnished teak cars set forth, each blazoned with the new name, Compagnie Internationale des Wagons-Lits et des Grands Express Européens, affectionately shortened to Madame La Compagnie. From Paris it ran to Strasbourg, Vienna, Budapest, and Bucharest, and then at Girugi in Romania passengers were ferried across the Danube and boarded cars provided by the Austrian Eastern Railway and went on to Varna, where they took the ferry on an eighteen-hour crossing of the Black Sea to Constantinople.

Apparently it wasn't the ordeal it sounds like today. In fact, it was an instant hit. By 1889 the track was completed to Constantinople and the journey was reduced to sixty-seven hours and thirty-five minutes of pure luxury.

World War I stopped the rolling train wheels and trapped many of the elegant carriages behind enemy lines. Then, in the Russian Revolution, Madame la Compagnie lost 161 cars that had been on the St. Petersburg or Trans-Siberian runs.

On November 11, 1918, the German surrender was officially received and the armistice signed. The ceremony took place in the most famous Wagon-Lits car of all, dining car 2419, which had been shunted onto a siding in the Forest of Compiégne, northeast of Paris.

When France fell in 1940, Hitler had 2419 hauled back to the exact spot of the earlier humiliation (they say he broke into an exultant dance beside it) and received the French surrender at the same table. Then he took 2419 back in triumph to Berlin.

In 1945 an SS unit blew it up to keep it from hosting a third surrender.

After World War I, under the terms of the Versailles treaty, the Orient Express was to shun disgraced Germany and Austria and use the Simplon Tunnel, which ran through the Alps between Brig and Domodossola and had carried the Simplon Express from Paris to Venice since 1906. Now the Orient Express became the Simplon Orient Express, going by way of Dijon, Lausanne, the tunnel, Milan, Venice, Trieste, Zagreb, Belgrade, Nish, and Sofia to Constantinople. The new route took fifty-six hours, and for the next nineteen years the train radiated its full glory.

The elite Golden Arrow and the Flèche d'Or carried English passengers from London to the Orient Express in Paris. In 1936 the Night Ferry made it possible to cross the channel sound asleep and join the Orient Express without stepping off the train, transported in glorious idleness from Victoria Station to the Bosporus.

The 1920s saw the most elegant of the coaches built, each unique interior a rolling work of art. The continental cars had numbers only, but the British-built Pullmans had romantic names – *Ibis, Ione, Minerva, Perseus,* and elegant *Cygnus* with the mosaic of Leda and the swan on the lavatory floor. There were art deco marquetry panels of landscapes; there were friezes, inlays, medallions, goddesses, garlands, and nude maidens dancing with bunches of grapes. Food and wine were consumed on a scale that sounds obscene to today's Puritans.

Not that every journey was a champagne dream. In 1929 the Orient Express was caught in a snowstorm sixty miles from Constantinople (soon to be Istanbul) and stood buried in drifts for nine days. The food ran out; the pipes froze. Turkish peasants trudged through the snow from their villages to sell bread to the trapped passengers, who washed it down with snow melted over a boiler on the locomotive – hardly the advertised menu. A plow sent to the rescue on the tenth day derailed and had to be righted. Presumably even the champagne ran out during the long ordeal.

The Depression of the 1930s bit into the luxury travel market, and then World War II once again halted the train. Tracks and the fairy-tale carriages were damaged or destroyed by bombs – or used to transport troops, which can't have been much easier on the inlaid marquetry. Sleeping car 3544, chosen for its large and exquisitely paneled lavatory, became a brothel in Limoges.

After the war some of the cars were salvaged and service was resumed, but plane travel was faster and cheaper and passengers defected. The Orient Express still seemed the dignified setting for occasions like Bulganin and Khrushchev's state visit to London in 1956, de Gaulle's in 1960, and Winston Churchill's funeral in 1965, but state visits can't support a railroad. The Iron Curtain complicated the troubles, descending over stretches of the route.

Gradually the great train, former darling of the world's famous, deteriorated until, in 1977, it limped into Istanbul on its last run, four cars long, seven hours late, and carrying no restaurant car. Passengers had brought their own food.

Later in the year, in Monte Carlo, Sotheby's held an auction of five Orient Express cars that had appeared in the movie *Murder on the Orient Express*, based on the Agatha Christie book. The English entrepreneur James B. Sherwood was outbid on some by the King of Morocco, but he did buy two sleeping cars that would form the nucleus of his Venice-Simplon-Orient-Express.

For years he tracked down and restored the grand old cars, and in May 1982 the new train hit the tracks. It's actually two trains, the chocolate-and-cream-colored Pullman parlor cars, once part of the Golden Arrow, from London to Folkestone, and across the channel the dark-blue wagons-lits cars of the continent.

Once a week from March till November it pampers the nostalgic on its abbreviated run, rather like a landlocked cruise ship. It goes only from London to Venice and back. But any tourist can go to Venice. Riding to Constantinople with Mata Hari and Crown Prince Rudolph – that took glamor.

Glamor requires the support of what used to be called the Leisure Class, and nowadays the rich seem more interested in work than in play. Their idea of luxury travel is probably a conveniently outfitted limousine to whisk them from appointment to appointment, laptops on their laps.

Hardly the kind of journeying that inspires daydreams of glory in the rest of us.

THE WOMAN WHO FLEW AWAY

BASICALLY, WHAT YOU ALREADY KNOW about Amelia Earhart is the important part – that she was a pilot who got in a plane one day to fly across the Pacific and vanished, poof. Vanishing made her famous. If she'd come home safe and sound with a suitcase full of grass skirts and coconuts, you would never have heard of her.

Amelia was born in Kansas in 1897, a time when lots of brassy little girls were springing up, especially west of the Mississippi, so they could be on hand for the Roaring Twenties. Her mother's family was highly respectable, all judges and minister and bankers, just the kind of background that prompts the young to jump into planes and fly away. She was crazy about her father, but face it, he wasn't much use. He worked for the railroads when he was sober enough.

As a child, Amelia was stubborn and impatient and secretive, and shot rats with a .22. She kept a scrapbook of clippings about women who did manly things, like running for mayor, and she was very pure and high-minded because she didn't care a fig for sex, which always helps.

She dropped out of college to be a nurse's aide in the Great War, as it was then called. Later she studied auto mechanics and the banjo, and went to Columbia as a pre-med student. Then she dropped out again and went to Los Angeles with her parents. She was tall and leggy and good-looking, with golden hair and nice gray eyes, but she thought marriage would tie her down and said wives were "domestic robots." What she needed was a calling in life, but nothing quite seemed to suit.

Then when she was twenty-three her father took her to the opening tournament of an airfield in Long Beach, and it simply swept her off her feet. She said she thought she'd just die if she couldn't learn to fly.

This turned out not to be necessary, and up she went.

No, she wasn't the first woman pilot. There were lots of them, though not as many as men, because the men had learned at taxpayers' expense during the war. This always griped Amelia, and she made a number of speeches about it, saying women ought to be drafted so they could fly for free. When the war was over, the government planes got sold off and the pilots got laid off and bought the planes and took up barnstorming, stunt flying, air circuses, and teaching Amelia. The skies were simply fluttering with wispy little patched-up crates made of linen and wood and bits of wire.

Her various instructors and colleagues differ on her talents. Some said she was "a natural," others that she was just awful. Even after she was famous, dear old flying friends murmured that she was klutzy and amateurish, and her landings and takeoffs could whiten the hair of spectators, not to mention passengers. Whenever she crashed, she always pointed out that it wasn't her fault. She was very clear about this, and explained that the sun was in her eyes, or she hit a puddle, or blew a tire, or something. She crashed often, but so did most people. In those days it didn't hurt as much as it does now. An amazing number of pilots didn't get killed at all, just climbed down out of the trees and brushed off the twigs.

Amelia became an airfield groupie, and hung out helping to shellac wings, replace struts, and buzz Malibu Beach. Naturally she wanted her own plane. To earn the money she bought an old truck and contracted to haul gravel in it. Presently her mother gave her the money on condition that she give up gravel-trucking, which was scandalizing the neighbors.

She bought a little Airster with one bad cylinder and a tendency to ground-loop in crosswinds and crash in cabbage patches, and painted it yellow and named it "Canary." Pretty soon she was flying in exhibitions. She set an altitude record at fourteen thousand feet in an open cockpit and lashings of sleet and fog; open cockpits were hard on the complexion but blew away the gas fumes. The gas fumes were the main reason everyone threw up every ten miles or so. Ah, those were the days.

She was strong and stubborn and she set quite a few records altogether; endurance was her forte. She was the first person to fly solo from Hawaii to California, and the first person to cross the Atlantic twice in a plane, and the first woman to fly across it solo, and to fly an autogiro, and to fly cross-country without stopping, and to win the National Geographic Society's gold medal.

It all started because a public-relations fellow noticed that she looked like Charles Lindbergh, who had flown across the Atlantic the year before, in 1927. She really did look like him. A Norwegian artist said she "looked more like Lindbergh than Lindbergh himself." George ("G. P.") Putnam, of Putnam's the publishers, who had made a bundle promoting Lindbergh, spotted her and decided he could make some more money if this "Lady Lindy" went across, too, so she did, and he did. The catch is that she wasn't flying the plane. She was sitting in back on the gas cans playing gin rummy with the mechanic, and as a personal achievement it ranks right up there with being the first white rat in orbit.

Wilmer Stulz was flying the plane. This was too bad as Wilmer, known as Bill, was drunk out of his mind and could hardly find the ocean, much less England. Some sources say he was *not* drunk, just hideously hungover, but that doesn't explain why Amelia had to haul him out of bed and half carry him to the plane because he couldn't walk, or why he smuggled a bottle on board. Somewhere over the Atlantic, they got so lost that when they saw the S.S. *America* down below, Amelia dropped a message tied to two oranges, asking for directions, but she missed and the oranges fell in the water.

Oddly enough, they finally spotted some land, and landed, but it turned out to be a place called Burry Port in Wales, 140 miles from Southhampton where the crowds waited to cheer. They were lucky to be *anywhere*. When they did get to London, they were wined and dined, and Amelia danced with the Prince of Wales and bought a single-engine Avro Avian. G. P. paid for it. He had plans for her.

Back home, she wrote a book for him called *20 Hrs. 40 Mins.: Our Flight in the "Friendship."* It was dull; how much can you write about gin rummy? Then she tried to fly the Avian to the West Coast and back, with various problems like cracking up in a ditch in Pittsburgh, and having to land on a street in Pecos, and belly-flopping in Yuma and again outside Salt Lake City. Every time she crashed she lost a lot of time waiting around for parts. (Nowadays when we crash we don't have to wait for parts. There are parts all over the place.) Wherever she came slamming into a town, everyone cheered and cut chunks of fabric from the plane's wings for her to autograph.

Back home, she became the aviation editor of Hearst's *Cosmopolitan* and wrote uninspiring articles for it. She really hated writing, but G. P. wouldn't let her stop. He was managing her career, and got her jobs endorsing soap and gasoline, and booked her for endless lecture tours. She lectured on the future of aviation, jobs for women, peace, and justice. People came swarming to see her, and she was a handsome sight; it wasn't necessary to listen.

Because buying planes is like eating peanuts, she bought a Lockheed Vega and flew in a women's cross-country race, rudely referred to as the Powder Puff Derby. She crashed in Yuma and again in Phoenix, but came in third because everyone else had similar troubles, and one was in the hospital and one was dead.

Aviation was here to stay. Commercial airlines were getting bigger, and adding conveniences like unlimited sickbags and rubber matting on the floor so it could be hosed down, but the cockpits were still guy country. Amelia got up an organization of women pilots to press for more jobs for women in commercial aviation, with, as one can see today, only so-so results.

Now G. P., who knew a cash cow when he saw one, kept proposing, and finally in 1931 she gave in and married him. It only took a couple of minutes, and afterward she went on with what she'd been saying about autogiros. She wasn't the bridal type. Anne Morrow Lindbergh once said of her, "She has a clarity of mind, impersonal eye, coolness of temperament, and balance as a scientist. Aside from that, I like her."

G. P. kept calling the wire services and newsreel people every time she left the house, but she hadn't broken any records lately and folks were getting jaded. She needed a newsworthy angle, so she took up autogiros, an embryonic form of helicopter used principally for killing pilots. Beech-Nut, the chewing-gum people, lent her theirs so she could fly across the country and back, stopping down eight or ten times a day to give out interviews and chewing gum. On the way back she dropped onto a couple of parked cars in Abilene. It wasn't her fault – autogiros were always falling from the sky like concrete ducks – but the authorities threatened to ground her for carelessness anyway.

Then she decided – or G. P. decided for her – to solo

across the Atlantic in the spring of '32, in a dark red Vega with gold and black stripes. First G. P. made her sit down and write a book about it, *For the Fun of It,* all except the last nine pages to be filled in after she got back. Then he picked the date, the fifth anniversary of Lindbergh's flight, and she took off from Newfoundland toward Paris with a toothbrush and a thermos of soup.

It was hardly any fun at all, even compared to dental surgery. She ran smack into a wicked storm, and when she tried to fly over it the whole plane turned to ice, and when she dropped back down she couldn't tell how close the waves were because the altimeter broke. So did the tachometer and the gas gauge. Gas dripped down her neck, and the manifold cracked and exhaust flames lit up the North Atlantic. When she saw a fishing boat at dawn, she figured land must be around somewhere, and whatever it was she'd better postpone Paris and head for it. It was northern Ireland, and she landed in a field and frightened the cows.

In London she was wined and dined and danced with the Prince of Wales again. Some of the press said her "glory shed luster on all womanhood." Some of it said she was vain and foolish and did it for publicity. The French gave her the Cross of the Legion of Honor. New York was all but buried in ticker tape. The National Geographic Society gave her a gold medal, as if she'd *discovered* Ireland instead of just bumping into it. Congress and the Cabinet cheered, and she had to eat dinner with President Hoover, part of the price of fame back then.

She quickly filled in the blank pages of *For the Fun of It,* and G. P. had it in the bookstores within a week. After buzzing out to California to get the Distinguished Flying Cross, she flew back nonstop for a cross-country distance record. (Fastidious women avoided long-distance flights because pilots' "relief tubes," as they were delicately called, weren't designed for women, so they just had to sit there and let nature take its course. Amelia didn't care.)

To G. P.'s delight, everyone wanted her to lecture to their groups and endorse their products, and he hardly gave her time to wash her hair. Her price had gone up until two lectures would buy a new Buick, and he had her booked morning, noon, and night. In her spare time, he arranged for her to design, model, and sell a line of fashions for active living.

She got to be great friends with the Roosevelts, who were president by now, and took Eleanor for a photo-op plane ride; Eleanor was inspired to take flying lessons, but FDR talked her out of it. He said they couldn't afford a plane.

With Eugene Vidal, father of Gore, she started an airline, the Boston & Maine, puddle-jumping through the north, and they got to be great pals; she always wore his jockey shorts when flying, for luck. Then this too began to pall, either on Amelia or on G. P.

She felt she'd made enough women's records and ought to try for a unisex record, Honolulu to San Francisco, alone in a single-engine plane over twenty-four hundred miles of open water. Everyone thought she was a raging idiot, and the military were seriously upset, but a public-relations deal was already in place, involving the price of sugar and Hawaiian statehood, so she went ahead. As always, G. P. insisted she take off on a Friday, weather or no weather, to arrive on Saturday in time to make the Sunday papers. He was a conscientious manager.

According to some, it was foggy, and she got seriously lost, since she never did know shucks about radio telegraphy or navigation. Others say it was clear and starlit and she navigated flawlessly by compass. Whichever, she made Oakland just two hours behind her ETA, unlike some planes. Roosevelt called her a trailblazer, but *Newsweek* said it was just a stunt to jack up her lecture prices. A British weekly said she was old enough to have better sense.

G. P. could only think of more of the same, and sent her off on another Friday for a Mexico City–Newark run. She got lost in Mexico and had to land in a dry lakebed and ask some cowboys how to get to Mexico City, but after that she found New Orleans and Newark, and was famous all over again.

Upping the ante in 1937, the next trip would be around the world at the Equator. Wiley Post had soloed around the world in 1933, but she was going to take a longer route and call it a new record. G. P. threw himself into the arrangements, pulling every string in sight. He got the Roosevelts to help with things like flight permits, and arranging for midair refueling over Midway so she could fly across four thousand miles of open water without even a nap. He got Purdue University to buy her a new plane, and bargained shrewdly for cheaper equipment and even a cheaper navigator, Fred Noonan.

Some sources say Noonan had positively *not* been fired

from Pan Am for drinking, but walked out under his own steam as a career move; other sources just laugh. The first sources say, anyway he was a perfectly good navigator when he was sober, and the other sources say, how would anyone know? Those inside the aviation world have wondered aloud why both Wilmer Stultz and Fred Noonan hadn't been permanently grounded for drinking long before they met Amelia. Amelia seemed to have a soft spot for drunks, perhaps because they smelled like her beloved father, but that seems a slender reason for flying across oceans with them.

Well, they got as far as Hawaii, and then Amelia cracked up her nice new two-engine Electra on takeoff and it had to go home in a box. Amelia went home on a ship. It made a nice change, with showers and toilets and hot meals. She and G. P. touched their friends for another fifty thousand dollars to fix the Electra, and then off she went again, complete with Noonan.

The arrangements involved finding and landing on an island in the Pacific called Howland, which was roughly the size of the Cleveland airport and thousands of miles from anything else except fish. If and when she found it, the American taxpayers had built her a nice landing strip. Some of her friends worried about her radio, which needed a 250-foot trailing booster wire they were sure she wouldn't bother to take along. They were right. Neither she nor Noonan knew a whole lot about radios anyway, and felt it probably wasn't necessary. She did take the telegraph transmitter, but left the key behind; neither of them could do Morse code, which would be much the best way of getting in touch, but they were seat-of-the-pants folks and proud of it.

On June 1 they took off from Miami, and G. P. was beside himself with despair because Wally Simpson married Edward of England the next day and hogged all the headlines.

Amelia flew down Brazil, and across the Atlantic, and over to Africa, where it was so hot they had to wait till dark to fuel the plane so the gas wouldn't catch fire. She was the first person to fly from the Red Sea across Arabia to Karachi, but *The New York Times* only gave it three sentences. Every time she phoned home G. P. yelled at her for more stories and film, and reminded her to be back by July Fourth, as he had lots of interviews and talk shows set up. She complained about airsickness and diarrhea and plane problems and "personnel trouble." Or she may have said "crew unfit," or "personnel unfitness." Accounts differ, and G. P. censored the press releases. Some sources say surely this didn't have anything to do with Noonan and the liquor cabinet, and no doubt she meant her own illnesses. They suggest she may have been pregnant, or menopausal. Maybe.

She'd flown twenty thousand miles in 135 hours, and the monsoon was pouring down. She did get to New Guinea, though, and then made a sloppy final takeoff into nowhere, clearing the bay at the end of the runway by a good five feet. A cruel rumor suggests that Noonan had had to be helped on board again, in no condition to know which direction they were going, but this may be totally unfounded.

The Pacific was full of ships and bases trying to keep track of her, but nobody knew how feeble her radio equipment was, and how she'd left its attachments in Miami. To make matters worse, it was the Fourth of July weekend already and she was missing the interviews G. P. had lined up.

Howland is 2,556 miles from New Guinea, and only two miles long by three-quarters of a mile wide. When she was already late arriving, she tuned in several times to ask Howland to take a bearing on her by radio, but she wouldn't talk long enough to get located and she never mentioned her position, or course, or speed, or ETA. Before she left, she'd been signed up to take a stiff course in radio procedures and operation, but had to leave for an appointment after an hour. She was, so to speak, winging it.

Howland kept listening for her through the static. Once she claimed to be circling them, but they couldn't hear anything. She must have been circling something else. Apparently she was flying under clouds, but the sky over Howland was clear.

At a quarter of nine, she asked for directions, and said, "We are running north and south." She'd been airborne for twenty-three hours, and she'd had twenty-three hours worth of gas.

For sixteen days four thousand men in ten ships and sixty-five planes combed the Pacific for her at great expense, and she was about as famous as a person can get.

She stayed famous, too. There were movies, and rumors, and speculations about how maybe she was a spy sent by the Roosevelts to check up on the Japanese, and how the Japanese had captured her and either executed her or let her die of dysentery. Or she wasn't captured, and reported back to Washington and was living in New Jersey under a new name. The Roosevelts and the Japanese denied everything, but for decades people kept claiming they'd found bits of her plane, or legends about her among the Pacific islanders.

She'd always said she wanted to die in her plane, and we assume she planned to keep trying till she got it right. Before she left, she'd said her greatest horror was of growing old, and she was already thirty-nine. "I won't feel completely cheated if I fail to come back," she said.

It cost the taxpayers a bundle, but it was a grand way to go. G. P. himself couldn't have planned it better.

Ice Cream
The Old, Cold Caress

WE WANT IT. We can't help ourselves. The voluptuous melting of cold, sweet spoonfuls on the tongue, the mix of rich decadence with icy purity, has held us in thrall for a long time.

In the first century A.D. the Emperor Nero, who had a taste for delicacies, ordered teams of runners sent to the Alps for snow. It was a month's journey back to Rome, and if the snow arrived intact, Nero ate it flavored with honey, nuts, and fruit juices. If it had dribbled away en route, all concerned were fed to the lions.

Flavored snow was our first sweet chill. In warm countries it was strictly for those rich enough to import it; by the sixteenth century, horsemen were racing from the Hindu Kush for the sorbets of Delhi, Turks were shipping it in from Bursa, and the Mexican emperor Montezuma had it backpacked down from the mountaintops and ate it drizzled with hot chocolate, thus inventing the hot fudge sundae.

Even the best of snow, however, is basically just fluffy

water. Apparently it was Marco Polo who brought home the breakthrough variation. The thirteenth-century wanderer came back to Venice from China with, besides gunpowder and other exotic toys, a recipe for a frozen cream that he said his hosts had served as a digestive after meals. Presumably the Chinese had discovered the trick of shaking up the ingredients as they froze, breaking down the ice crystals and pumping in air to fluff and soften it.

The cream, adding its buttery touch of sensuous luxury, was a real improvement over snow. Freezing it was no problem; Italians had been collecting and storing ice to chill the drinks of summer since ancient times. Christened *gelati,* iced cream was an instant hit with the upper classes.

In 1533 the young Catherine de Médicis moved from Florence to Paris to marry Henry II. She took along her chef, Bernardo Buontalenti, who took along gelati recipes, and the French joined in the fun.

Being French, they made creations. They colored it and molded it into elaborate architectural fantasies and played tricks with it. At one state dinner given by Louis XIV, dessert was apparently individual boiled, dyed Easter eggs, cold and hard as marble, throwing the guests into confusion until they politely spooned into them.

Across the Channel, Charles I considered "frozen cream ice" too good even for the lesser nobility and paid his French chef twenty pounds a year to keep the recipe a royal secret, or so the story goes. After Charles lost his head in 1649, a group of nobles got to the cook, bought his recipe, and spread it around.

In Paris, it became the rage at cafés like Tortoni's place,

which featured a rum-and-almond concoction that still bears the proprietor's name. In Vienna, it became a year-round way of life. Norway made a good thing out of shipping its extra ice all over Europe to freeze the spreading habit.

In America George Washington, that stern puritanical father figure, was almost alarmingly fond of it; in one summer alone he noted spending two hundred eighteenth-century dollars on ice cream and also owned – perhaps in an effort to economize – a "cream machine for making ice." This was probably a covered pewter canister in which the cream mix was shaken steadily in a bucket of salt and ice. (Labor-intensive, but Washington owned over three hundred slaves and didn't mind.)

Thomas Jefferson, a man as easily excited by food as he was by inventing gadgets, brought the Baked Alaska back from his stay in France, calling it an "Omelette Surprise" (the French used egg yolks in their ice cream). In France it was more commonly called *Omelette à la Norvégienne,* in honor of the Norwegian ice supplies that froze Europe's ice cream. Its later name was a sarcastic comment on the purchase of an unappreciated territory to our north.

This novelty has fallen out of favor, but for those who would like to invoke Jeffersonian banquets: line the baking dish with slices of spongy cake, top them with an oval mound of ice cream, and cover it with more strips of cake. Thoroughly smother the whole thing in a meringue of stiffly beaten egg whites and bake it under a five-hundred-degree broiler for three minutes, or until it just begins to color like a Siamese cat. Serve it, needless to say, promptly.

It wasn't until 1846 that the American Nancy Johnson invented the portable, hand-cranked ice cream maker so dear to rural memories. A canister set into a wooden tub of ice and salt held the cream mixture while it was beaten for twenty minutes or so by a hand-turned paddle. The idea is so close to the ancient, universal butter churn that it seems odd it took centuries to think of, but anyway, after its arrival, every household could make its own, and ice cream manufacturing became commercially thinkable.

In 1851, in Baltimore, Jacob Fussell, a milk dealer with seasonal cream surpluses, opened the first ice cream factory, which soon blossomed into an empire. Electric power replaced expensive hand cranking, prices dropped, and sales soared.

While the French experimented with brandy ice cream and rhubarb sherbet, America tinkered with the basics. At the St. Louis World's Fair in 1904, a vendor rolled thin waffles into cones and topped them with ice cream; soon summer strollers were licking and nibbling in the parks, followed by dogs hoping for an accidental bonanza. Eskimo Pies appeared, and Dixie Cups, chocolate and vanilla in a small box with a pull-off lid, to be eaten afoot with a wooden paddle.

Soda fountains flourished in drugstores, their marble counters an echo of the formal ice cream parlors, and survived into the 1950s, a refreshment pause for the shopping housewife and meeting place for the after-school crowd.

Recently a customer in an ice cream parlor asked for a soda and drew a blank look. "A scoop of vanilla ice cream, douse it with chocolate syrup, and drown it in soda water," she explained, adding dreamily, "It's served in a tall fluted glass with a long-handled spoon. You slurp up the dregs with a straw. . . ." The counterman said it sounded disgusting and she was probably mistaken; she must be thinking of a root beer float.

There were sundaes, too, born when religious groups decreed that sodas are too much fun to be sold on the Sabbath. Resourceful proprietors simply left out the soda and served the remains in a dish. (Originally "Sunday sodas," the name was respelled to avoid blasphemy.)

And there were milk shakes in tapered aluminum containers, buzzed into a froth on their special agitators. And the banana split, heaped high on its oval dish – bananas, three kinds of ice cream, fudge sauce, whipped cream, cherries, nuts – the pinnacle of soda-fountain gourmandise.

As an alternative indulgence, ice cream got a boost from Prohibition, and its manufacturers produced a song about Daddy's wholesome new habit: "He brings a brick of ice cream home instead of beer."

In the 1920s the Good Humor truck, product of marketing genius Harry Burt, jingled onto the scene. Children too young for the soda-fountain scene clustered around the white-coated driver and exchanged their nickels for vanilla on a stick, coated with chocolate that flaked off onto the wrists of slow eaters.

When other marketing geniuses replaced Burt, the young replaced ice cream with hamburgers, once the amateur's boring supper on cook's night out, as their fun food of choice.

Grown-ups moved in to fill the ice cream vacuum. Gone was the vision of ice cream as stripes of chocolate, strawberry, and vanilla melting on a paper plate at a birthday party. Ice cream went sophisticated; one study shows American adults now eat three times as much of it as children do. This accounts for the rise of the pricey, premium, too-good-for-the-kids ice cream, the kind that hefts so weightily in the hand, being more cream than air, and reads so reassuringly. "Fresh cream," it says; "sugar, yolk of egg, natural vanilla." Who wants to eat the whey protein concentrate, guar gum, and sodium alginate of lesser brands?

Under federal regulations, if you're going to sell it as ice cream it has to be made with cream and contain at least 10 percent butterfat. Some premium brands have 16 percent or more, giving them that wickedly voluptuous caloric caress on the tongue. In general, the more expensive the brand, the shorter and simpler the table of contents; regulations allow twelve hundred ingredients and additives, some of them unpronounceable, and the lowliest brands are rich mainly in chemicals and light as a feather.

The two basic types of ice cream are "French," made with egg yolks and more milk than cream, and "Philadelphia," made with no egg and more cream than milk. Sherbets and sorbets were originally slushy, fruit-flavored drinks rather than food, and popular in hot countries and as a refresher between courses or after dinner. Technically, sherbet is made with fruit and egg whites, milk, or gelatin, and sorbet with frozen fruit juice or puree and sugar water. Frozen yogurt is held by the nutritionally correct to be

more wholesome than ice cream, but its virtues, after pro-
cessing and additives, have been seriously compromised.

At first glance, ice cream seems a peculiar passion for a
nation so famously preoccupied with losing weight. Not
that it's really so fat making – less so than a hamburger,
anyway, unless we eat the whole pint – but we think of it
as oozing wicked calories. Stendhal said, after his first
taste, "What a pity this isn't a sin," and now, in our thin-
obsessed, anti-cholesterol times, we've managed to make
it one.

Maybe that's the point. Maybe, after all those carrot
sticks, when we go off our diets we want to do it right. Not
with humble pork chops or pancakes but with a sinful,
sensuous binge on our classic indulgence, our old, cold
love.

Even the portly Nero put plenty of honey on his snow.

Twelve Good Men and True

O, will you swear by yonder skies
Whatever question may arise,
'Twixt rich and poor, 'Twixt low and high,
That you will well and truly try?
                    Gilbert & Sullivan, "Trial by Jury"

WHEN LAW AND ORDER BEGAN, the only court was the head
of the family group, and father knew best. His word was
law and there was no appeal. If papa was a bully, maybe
mama could pack up the kids and move to a different
family. Or spike his soup with the leaves and berries her
mother told her about. In any case, what happened in the
family was nobody's business but the family's.

Presently people developed agriculture and settled down,
clustering together in groups of families. We acquired garden plots and portable private property, and controversy
as we know it was born. Old Paterfamilias still decided
family matters, but coping with interfamilial strife called
for group arbitration to prevent a homicidal free-for-
all. (Or try to prevent it; the human animal has a natural
taste for homicidal free-for-alls.) Controversy gave birth
to law.

Law is an ever-deepening pile of decisions that, once
made, become permanent. This is a great time-saver. If it's
wrong for A to steal B's battle-axe on Tuesday, then it's

automatically wrong for C to steal D's battle-axe on Wednesday, whether the matter is written down or just preserved as remembered usage. We don't need to thrash it out over and over again.

We do need to find out whether C really stole the axe, or if D just lost the thing and blamed it on C. To establish this, we check with the neighbors. Is D a famous liar? Does he have a grudge against C? Has anyone seen C chopping up Saxons with the axe? These folk are witnesses. If we find the axe under C's bed, that's evidence.

The laws are established, facts discovered, witnesses heard, and judgment made. These functions have been separated in our fancier world, but in the early tribunals they were all one. The group called in to consider the matter was made up of witnesses; if no law already applied to the case, they made one that would; they talked it over and decided.

They were all amateurs. Laws were so simple that ordinary folk could understand them. Now professionals have taken over the courts and, I hear, get well paid for it, but juries are still amateurs called in for the occasion, unattached to the system. The good thing about juries is that they're amateurs. The bad thing about juries is that they're amateurs.

Rome refined the system and separated the law from the facts. A magistrate defined the dispute, cited the law, and referred the problem to a citizen *judex* – a fellow of some standing – who called in associates to help. They listened to the speeches, weighed the evidence, and pronounced sentence. (Nobody was supervising them, so it helped if one of them was a lawyer, to explain.) This was more orderly than tribunals. The Romans were passionately fond of order and wrote down all their laws in books.

They were also fond of a good public spectacle, and a convicted criminal could opt for the arena and entertain the citizens by duking it out with other criminals or prisoners of war. A talented gladiator not only got to live; he could wind up a popular sports hero, surrounded by pretty ladies. The Romans loved a winner, regardless of his criminal record.

Meanwhile, the Scandinavians were gathering regularly in tribunals, called *Things,* dating back further than anyone remembered. Groups of delegates met to represent their districts, and committees of twelve, or multiples of twelve, were picked to administer or invent the laws.

Twelve is the solemn number. When Morgan of Gla-Morgan, king of Wales, established trial by jury in 725 A.D., he wrote, "For as Christ and his twelve apostles were finally to judge the world, so human tribunals should be composed of the king and twelve wise men." Maybe. Or maybe Christ was following an older tradition. The number twelve crops up all over. The zodiac has twelve signs, based on twelve constellations; we divide our days into twice-twelve hours; twelve midnight rings in the witching hour. We buy our eggs by the dozen and undertake semi-mystical cures in twelve steps. Scandinavian folk tales offer us twelve princesses, trolls with twelve heads, and twelve princes changed into twelve wild ducks.

Maybe twelve has ancient powers. After all, the opinion of eleven jurors is merely an opinion, but the opinion of twelve is magic, transforming the presumed innocent into the guilty like a prince turned into a frog.

So the Scandinavians gathered and chose up groups of twelve. (Back then, as now, the parties could object if they spotted their archenemy or their victim's glowering father among the twelve.) They swore to vote justly and then decided the matter according to what seemed to them natural rightness.

It's pleasant to think of them meeting century after century for this civilized rite of community justice, a society taking responsibility for its common good conduct. Unfortunately, northern Europe doesn't remember the Norsemen as calm, thoughtful, reasonable fellows; the *Things* may have been as uproarious in practice as they were virtuous in principle. Heads may have cracked.

After Rome fell apart, her former empire went all to sixes and sevens and her orderly laws decayed into gibberish. In Britain, the possibly legendary King Arthur had to send his possibly legendary knights out to ride around righting wrongs and rescuing maidens from sexual harassment, a far from comprehensive justice system. There were still trials, though, with the ordeal serving as jury.

Great faith has been placed in trial by ordeal, all the way from the Old Testament to the Australian outback. The idea is that *something out there* knows who's guilty and will point to him if given a chance. The chance usually involves fire or water or poison.

Poison was recommended in the Bible and popular in Africa and Brahmanic India for trials by ordeal: those who survived at all, though likely to be ill, were considered innocent. The Saxons developed a variation called "corns-naed," a morsel of something that would choke the guilty – perhaps their throats were dry with apprehension. Godwin, Earl of Kent, is said to have choked on his.

Under Saxon law, if you could carry several pounds of glowing red-hot iron in your bare hands for nine steps or walk barefoot over nine red-hot plowshares without getting blisters, you weren't guilty. Similar proof was accepted in Hindu and Scandinavian law. In Britain, Africa, and parts of Asia, plunging your arm into boiling water, oil, or lead without the usual results proved your innocence.

Water was also knowledgeable stuff. The innocent sank; the guilty floated, and could be fished out and dealt with. This was the customary method of identifying witches, who were cross-tied thumb-to-toe before being thrown in. True witches refused to drown and were dried off and burned at the stake.

Alongside this undignified jurisprudence, the Saxons were actually working out a human jury system, but it was available only to the honest. If your neighbors knew you for a liar, or you'd perjured yourself in the past, or, presumably, if you were a stranger just passing through, you weren't "oath-worthy" and went directly to the red-hot iron or the drowning-pond. But if you were a person of known honesty in your district and were accused of a crime, you swore, "By the Lord, I am guiltless both in deed and counsel of the charge of which X accuses me," and that was that. However, if you were accused by a group, you had to parry with a group of your own, called "compurgators." You asked eleven thanes – freeholders – to join you and swear to your honesty in the matter. If you couldn't round up eleven who believed you, you took off your shoes for the hot ploughshares.

In those days, honesty was the best policy. Honesty, and a loyal group of bribable drinking buddies. Ethelred, noticing this flaw, provided for a group of twelve senior thanes to investigate and act as an accusatory jury; eight votes could convict.

Justice was still a neighborhood matter. Everyone was supposed to know everyone else and have some first-hand knowledge of what happened. Rather recently, we've turned this concept on its head and juries are supposed to know nothing at all before they sit down in the box; to be but as empty vessels into which the liquor of admissable evidence is poured. In inflammatory cases, the trial even gets moved to another area to ensure the jurors' indifference.

The television in every room makes it harder to find jurors sufficiently isolated to qualify; jurors too listless to turn the TV on, too apathetic to have an opinion, and too morose even to lend an ear at the water-cooler. (Nobody's actually proved that ignorance promises fairness. In fact, a study of English trials between 1550 and 1750 showed that juries overwhelmingly acquitted the people they knew and convicted passing strangers.)

A seventeenth-century prisoner complained that one of the jurors was a dear friend of the prosecutor, and the judge snapped, "And do you challenge a juryman because he is supposed to know something of the matter? For that reason the juries are called from the neighborhood, because they should not be wholly strangers to the fact."

In Saxon times, a nosy curiosity about the neighbors was required by law. A regulation sometimes credited to King Alfred (not to be confused with the possibly legendary Arthur) in the ninth century divided everyone into groups or "tythings" of ten families, who were all held responsible for each other's behavior. Canute's law read, "And we will that every freeman be brought into a hundred, and into a tything." Nonmembers were outlaws; members, called "hundredors," oversaw law and order and each other's personal lives. In murder cases, if they didn't produce a culprit within a month and a day they all paid a fine. Every man was his brother's keeper. This made life simpler for the police, but it seems to be an idea whose time has gone.

The hundreds were democratic, mixing the washed and the unwashed and giving the latter a voice. The county court, presided over by the sheriff, met every six months, and twelve-man juries chosen for their personal knowledge of the case decided matters concerning their hundred. Below the county court was the court of the hundred, convened every four weeks as a local police court, keeping order and protecting rights, its juries sworn to "accuse no innocent man, nor conceal any guilty one." Disgruntled parties could appeal to the king.

Folks back then were so primitive that they thought the victim, rather than the law, had been damaged, and bodily harm was redeemed at so much for a finger, so much for an ear, all the way up to murder, which, in Alfred's time, cost two hundred shillings, payable to the deceased's family.

(Among the Germans it was payable in sheep.) Thieves paid the value of the stolen object plus a fine; repeat offenders and those who stole from the church paid with a hand or a foot as well.

This would mean that if someone broke your arm while stealing your car, he paid for your arm, *and* your car, *and* you got to keep the fine and possibly his foot too. Now he just goes to jail, and you get to pay for his room and board with taxes. Progress has been made.

When William the Conqueror took over England in 1066, he left the Saxon system in place and added some Norman flourishes, like trial by combat. Combat was a judicial entertainment similar to the gladiatorial, in which right makes might, so the winner must be right. The accuser had to do battle with the accused, causing the small and frail to think twice before complaining, but if you were no good at fighting you could hire someone to fight for you. The man with the fiercest hired help won – rather like hiring the most expensive lawyer today.

Ordeals fell into disuse in the thirteenth century, but the right to trial by combat stayed on the books until *Ashford* v. *Thornton* in 1819.

By Norman times laws were more complicated, so professionals, called "justiciars," were sent around to keep an eye on the courts and the rules of evidence, rather like judges. They knew more about the law and less about what had happened than the jurors did.

We were told in school that jury trials sprang newborn from the Magna Carta, but juries were around before 1215. Magna Carta just guaranteed them as a right not to be ignored by capricious powers like Bad King John, but some kings went right on being capricious anyway. In these enlightened times, we merely torch the neighborhood if we don't like the verdict, but back then juries got punished if the authorities didn't like it. Since juries were still considered witnesses, a wrong vote was considered perjury. Acquitting unpopular or possibly treasonous people got jurors hauled into the Star Chamber, where a group of the king's dear friends dealt severely with them. They lost their goods and chattels and went to jail for at least a year; sometimes their wives and children were thrown out of their houses, the houses demolished, the meadows destroyed, and even the trees chopped down. A prudent jury weighed factors other than the evidence. (It was also the custom for the winner to pay each juror several guineas and take them all out to dinner.)

Jurors, being human, and therefore cantankerous, occasionally voted their consciences anyway. Sometimes they even voted against the law. Juries have always given justice a bit of purely human wiggle-room. If they don't buy into the law as written, they can pummel it into shape, and a law under which nobody gets convicted eventually starves to death.

In 1650, under Cromwell, a newly reinstated law called for hanging adulteresses – and scarcely an adulteress was found in the land. In 1670, William Penn was tried for preaching Quaker doctrine; he couldn't have been guiltier, caught red-handed, and it was far from a first offense. The jurors stubbornly found in his favor and were fined forty marks apiece for wrongness. Four of them refused to pay and spent a year in prison, until one was brought before the court on *habeas corpus,* and lo, it was decided that the law couldn't jail jurors for their decisions.

We can't put them in jail anymore, but we can select them half to death.

As we limp toward the twenty-first century, the rural community of nosy neighbors has faded into history, and the problem now is, who *are* these jurors? King Morgan called them "wise men." Under Edward I, they were to be twelve of the "better men" of the bailiwick. Under George IV, "good and lawful men." (Except for adulteresses, witches, and common scolds, legal history doesn't mention women; perhaps they're a recent invention.) It seems to have been so simple then, naming our good, wise, lawful peers. But how do we choose among strangers not necessarily wise but merely registered to vote?

Once the blatantly prejudiced have been sent packing, both sides take up the peremptory challenge; turning down jurors for the way they look, dress, or comb their hair. A new professional has sprung up among us, the jury-selection consultant. For the O. J. Simpson trial, consultants submitted an eighty-page list of two hundred and ninety-four questions for prospective jurors, including essay questions like "What do you think is the main cause of domestic violence?" The theory is that we ordinary citizens are such a bunch of sheep that we'll always vote according to our kind, regardless of the evidence. The more narrowly the consultants can identify our kind, the easier it is to predict the vote.

The differing agendas of the prosecution and the defense complicate matters.

Prosecution lawyer Jeffrey Toobin says he was always told to avoid men with beards (too independent), teachers and social workers (too sympathetic), and aim for "the little old Lutheran lady in pearls, quick to judge and slow to forgive."

For the defense, Clarence Darrow advised not to "take a German; they are bull-headed. Rarely take a Swede; they are stubborn. Always take an Irishman or a Jew; they are the easiest to move to emotional sympathy." He preferred old men, for their tolerance. But Samuel Leibowitz liked them young, for their still-fresh sense of brotherhood; he avoided self-made men, businessmen with close-set eyes, writers, professors, and former policemen.

In his recent book, *We, the Jury*, Jeffrey Abramson recommends a patchwork, arguing that the soul of the jury rises out of its diversity; as people of various ages, classes and backgrounds rub their conflicting viewpoints together, the alchemy of a "collection of wisdom" shapes a consensus that represents us, the people. (Whether we're level-headed enough to deserve representation is another matter. Recently an English jury convicted in a murder case after receiving a message from the deceased on a smuggled Ouija board. But hey, we're all we've got.)

Abramson, anyway, has faith. He even agrees with Chief Justice John Marshall that it's all right for jurors to have read the newspapers.

Whatever it reads or watches, the modern jury doesn't know what it was designed to know – its neighbors – and a clever lawyer can sometimes play on it as upon a harp. Such was William Howe of Howe and Hummel, defender of the underworld in rowdy post–Civil War New York. Howe was an enormous, lion-headed man with a wardrobe of costumes for his courtroom performances and a talent for crying copiously over any case, however dull. Once he delivered a lengthy summation kneeling before the jury. Once he convinced a jury that his client's trigger finger had accidentally slipped, not once, but six times. So many of his clients were forgers that his office accepted only cash, so many were thieves that the office safe contained nothing but a coal scuttle, but murderers were his meat and drink.

He personally appeared for over six hundred and fifty of them. He virtually invented "temporary insanity." He wept; the jury wept. According to a newspaper account, during his defense of Annie Walden, The Man-Killing Race-Track Girl, "the sobs of juror nine could have been heard in the corridors, and there was moisture in the eyes of all but one or two of the other jurors."

Howe kept a stable of white-haired mothers, distraught wives, and sweet-faced children available to represent the family of the accused. He once pointed out his own wife and child, who happened to be in court, as his client's prospective widow and orphan. How would a New York jury know? And how the hometown juries of old would have laughed.

Here and there a voice suggests returning at least minor offences to neighborhood judicial counsels, as in the old courts of the hundreds. Taking the law into our own hands where it began. This may be utopian. We don't want to know our ninety-nine nearest neighbors, let alone be accountable for their behavior. Some of us don't even want to read the papers.

We gripe about the results, but we leave civil order to the professionals. It wasn't designed to work that way.

British lawyers tell the story of a jury in New South Wales considering the matter of some stolen cows, about which the jurors certainly knew more than the court would ever learn. After deliberating, they returned a verdict of "Not guilty, if he returns the cows." The judge was outraged at this insult to the law and threw them back out to think again. Pig-headed and mutinous, they returned with a new verdict, "Not guilty – and he doesn't have to return the cows."

Perhaps justice, if not law, was served.

ELVIS LIVES

IN 1993 THE SMITHSONIAN INSTITUTION, watchdog of America's cultural and historical reality, threw a party for Elvis. The party celebrated the opening of the National Postal Museum and, in recognition of the recent Elvis stamp, it was billed as "Mailhouse Rock." According to the bulletin, it featured live rock 'n' roll "and a special guest appearance by the King himself."

The bulletin did not explain or qualify. It didn't say they'd hired an Elvis impersonator for the evening. The Smithsonian, always a stickler for accuracy, officially expected Elvis, not driving a Caddie down the dark highways around Memphis but singing in the stately Flag Hall of the National Museum of American History.

That clinches it. Elvis Presley, who died in August of 1977, will not stay buried. Elvis walks. Of all the heroes and icons we've lost over the years, this is the most restless, the most persistent, the most unquiet revenant. What keeps him here?

Reassurance, maybe. The ego of the man who, at five-foot-eleven, had lifts built into all his shoes, was huge but fragile. When he was snubbed by the Grand Ole Opry and told to go back to driving a truck, he cried all the way home. Even at his pinnacle, the fastest-risen star in history was never sure of his welcome when he stepped on stage, and eventually came to believe that his fans must resent the millions they paid him and possibly want to kill him.

Fame was, ultimately, what he had; it was all he had left. At the time of his death, his was the second-most-recognized image in the world, after Mickey Mouse, and maybe he comes back to see if we still remember.

We do. Graceland is a well trampled shrine. Traveling museums display his clothes to respectful throngs as if they were the Shroud of Turin. According to *Harper's* Index, between 1991 and 1993 the number of *New York Times* stories mentioning Elvis jumped by 50 percent, and Elvis with Nixon is the most-requested photograph in the National Archives. Now the Postal Service and the Smithsonian have held out the one fruit fame denied him in his previous life – respectability. If he's here to count the house, to see if he's still the King, he must be satisfied.

Of course, he might simply be lonely. The man who led such a reclusive life from the age of twenty-three nevertheless had a horror of being alone, ever, even in the bathroom. He lived wrapped in a protective web of family hangers-on and the cronies who came to be called the Memphis Mafia, combining the functions of live-in staff, bodyguards, gofers, toadies, and freeloaders. (Sometimes, at dinner, they all sang "What a Friend We Have in Elvis.") Among their duties was shopping for girls in the mass of gathered fans and bringing their selections to the King; one night's head count came up with 152 dates for Elvis and seven henchmen. The epicenter of the endless party spent most of the night watching television, while his guests watched him watching.

Hardly the friendships that feed the soul. One day late in the sixties his Ferrari refused to start; he jumped out and pulled a brace of guns and emptied them into its body. In reply to a startled crony, he said, "I got pressures, man. I've got a demanding family, an expensive life, and I'm lonesome."

Cynics may find it hard to sympathize with a man who can afford to gun down his own Ferrari; others may flinch at the frantic tension behind the impulse. He had no gift for intimacy. His dangerously close attachment to his mother, and her early death, may have warped it, and very likely affected his marriage. He drew a fierce line between sex and motherhood, and as soon as his wife, Priscilla, announced her pregnancy he ended their physical relationship. She was drawn into an affair with her karate instructor and the Presleys eventually divorced, though Elvis continued to see his adored daughter, Lisa Marie, one of the few people he was able to love.

Perhaps he's still looking: "The grave's a fine and private place / But none, I think, do there embrace."

And then again, he was a lifelong sleepwalker and insomniac. (It was probably his insomnia that led to the drugs; downers at bedtime, then uppers to shake them off.) It's possible that he's here because, as always, he simply can't fall asleep.

But he has more compelling reasons for restlessness. He'd had a blazing natural talent – explosive, creative, inventive – that started a revolution and gave America her first true musical identity. "Before Elvis, there was nothing," John Lennon said. Elvis's high-spirited synthesis of gospel, rhythm-and-blues, and country-and-western slammed onto the scene and changed the sound of music. In the blandly sanitized years of Ike, his venereal stage rhetoric was, as one middle-aged survivor fondly remembers, "just outrageously sexy." His originality struck the world a shuddering jolt and then, through bad decisions, bad management, and crippling contracts, it dribbled away into the silly movies and stupefyingly repetitive shows in Las Vegas that made him a joke.

He wasn't paying attention. He didn't understand the complex of causes that bent his life downward, but he knew he'd lost something worth coming back to look for. He knew he'd missed the point.

He was not a stupid man.

He'd come a long way. His father was an illiterate, tobacco-chewing racist who'd done time in jail. Occasionally he drove a truck, but when Elvis started making money he retired forever at thirty-eight to devote his days to chasing women. His mother was superstitious, with a fondness for booze, diet pills, and snuff; her only other interest was Elvis.

We can argue that he didn't come far enough. We can fault him for his failure to develop musically, explore his powers, take charge of his career, or even look at contracts before signing them; to learn to read music and write his own songs or play that guitar he kept brandishing. (He told a reporter he didn't know a sharp from a flat: "In my kind of music you just get out there and go crazy.") He'd learned what he'd learned from listening to the radio – the family didn't own a record player – and always avoided give and take with his peers, the lessons and jam sessions and challenges. He'd been a C student in a vocational high school, listlessly majoring in shop, and nothing in his family traditions or personal experience opened the idea of sustained, purposeful study.

If he'd had to struggle his reach might have widened, but a year out of high school he was famous, girls screamed with rapture at the Snarlin' Darlin', and his career froze like a rabbit in the spotlight of the adolescent moment.

He'd never wanted to be a great musician. He wanted to be rich and famous – it was all he knew how to want – and he was. It's absurd for pious analysts to complain that we sacrificed him on the altar of American commercial entertainment; he'd thrown himself on that altar. In 1971 the Junior Chamber of Commerce gave him a trophy as one of the Ten Outstanding Young Men in America, and in his acceptance speech he said, "Every dream I ever dreamed has come true a hundred times."

Maybe even then, the statement gave him qualms. Remember, he was not a stupid man.

He bought nearly four hundred cars, some of them, like the Gold Car that was sent out alone on tour, so gaudily customized he couldn't drive them through the traffic jams they caused. He had a four-engine jet fitted out like a hotel's imperial suite and wore jewelry so immense it all but swallowed him. He said himself, when he was thirty-four, that he knew his hobbies were childish, but he'd dreamed a lot about *stuff* when he was a poor kid and now he was catching up.

He's had time enough to suspect that there was stuff he didn't know to dream about.

His analysts also complain that, with fame, he lost touch with his roots, but at least he never falsified them. In person, if not musically, he stayed hillbilly. Good taste was rampant in the land in those self-conscious years and people who didn't have it, if they could afford it, bought it. Elvis could have hired decorators to fill Graceland with real antiques instead of tacky fakes and waterfalls, and paint its walls ivory instead of tufting them with artificial suede. He could have hired a dealer to buy him Post-Impressionists. He could have learned, as the rest of us were learning, to eat French food with the right wines, but he went on eating banana-and-peanut-butter sandwiches with Coke. He stayed honest. Vulgar, yes; pretentious, never.

Perhaps honesty is at the root of his appeal. Even his most contrived performances have something honest at the heart; a flash of contact and complicity. In his rare taped interviews he's generally awkward and shy or sullen, but occasionally we catch sight of the wit, the half-smothered intelligence, and spontaneous charm of a high order that surprises unbelievers. Clearly there's a sweetness in him – "tremendously sweet," Natalie Wood called him – that feels authentic.

It's disconcerting to think that under the heavy, airtight ten-thousand-dollar-suit of real gold leaf there was an actual person, trapped, sweating, bored, and dismayed by his own dreams.

One place Elvis is never sighted is in a video store renting *Blue Hawaii* or any of its spinoffs. He called them travelogues. At times, as in *Viva Las Vegas* while driving the winning car in the climactic race, he looks poleaxed by such boredom as takes the breath away.

He might rent *Jailhouse Rock* for the stylish and witty staging of the title song, or *King Creole* for his rather sleepily Brandoesque performance; at least these were real movies with real, if corny, plots and no bevies of beach beauties. But given the way he came to feel about Hollywood, he's probably in a record store instead.

He may be looking for the early songs on the Sun label, back before he signed with RCA. Musicians keep them around; they cherish tapes of even the outtakes and alternate takes. They listen to the soaring, joyful freshness that was so easy and spontaneous and new, and they marvel at the man who was – and is – Elvis.

If you see him, say hello. Get an autograph. Tell him we haven't forgotten. Nobody here has forgotten.

Afterword

THIS IS A PECULIARLY uneven collection, representing my most recent years out of decades of writing to earn a living. Some of the pieces I wanted to write. Some I was told to write. Different publications called for different styles. They all paid me money.

I have read treatises explaining that no American writer needs to worry about the rent any more, or the children's shoes, or gas for the car, since all of us are comfortably supported by grants and universities and workshops and seminars where we either teach or hang out "in residence" or just collect the check, and this is a splendid thing. American writers are free at last, to write what they please, when they please, their creative juices unleashed from the children's milk-money.

Those of us who hover around, as it were, under the radar and out of the loop, feel suitably humble. We who never got channeled into the mainstream or handed through mentors into the universities and the literary community – those of us who bounced out of high school to cadge a living writing advertising copy and magazine fiction and press releases and mail-order catalogues, whose parents either couldn't or wouldn't poke us upward into the literary world – cast down our eyes before the sanctioned writers who were cushioned from the get-go. Needing money, we are obviously unworthy of money.

Still, it's been fun. No established literary personage will ever recognize my name; I shall never be invited to a party of the literati, or telephoned by one of their agents or publishers, but I've had a grand time. Being frivolous, I shall never make my scholarly mark. I get bored easily. A magazine article or a book that takes a year or less to research, that's me. Assignments to learn five thousand words about the history of juries, the Folies-Bergères, Columbus, Robin Hood, the Railroad Barons, apples, Mata Hari, Charlemagne, ice cream, Katharine Hepburn, Manifest Destiny, and Elvis Presley have made me very happy. My only requirement is that I not know anything about it to begin with, because why bother to learn if you already know? How can people trudge through life as specialists, already knowing, elaborating, rehashing, always in the same company? Is it worth the boredom, having one's rent paid?

I met a woman who had just finished the definitive biography of an eighteenth-century, under-biographied composer. It was about to go to press, to be simultaneously published in, I think, five countries. It had taken her thirteen years to research. It was a major, recognized, landmark achievement.

I still have nightmares about this woman who thought about the same thing for thirteen years. I wonder what's happened to her? Did she, when the book came out, find there was nothing left of her own life and just disappear?

So consider these pieces the product of financial necessity wed to a low boredom threshold.

Barbara Holland
Bluemont, Virginia